THE USBORNE BOOK OF
PEOPLES
OF THE
WORLD

(INTERNET-LINKED)

Gillian Doherty and Anna Claybourne

Designed by Laura Fearn and Linda Penny

Additional contributors: Nathalie Abi-Ezzi,
Kamini Khanduri and Rebecca Treays
Managing editor: Felicity Brooks
Managing designer: Stephen Wright
Cover design: Neil Francis
Digital image processing: John Russell and Mike Olley
Picture research: Ruth King
Cartographic editors: Craig Asquith
and Christine Johnston

Consultants:
Professor Michael Hitchcock, University of North London
Dr. Uwem Ite, Department of Geography, University of Lancaster
Susan Bermingham, M.A, Head of Humanities,
Royton and Crompton School, Oldham
Dr. Stephanie Bunn, University of Manchester
Dr. Susan Pfisterer, Menzies Centre for Australian Studies,
King's College, University of London
Dr. Vivien Miller, Senior Lecturer in American Studies, Middlesex University
Dr. Francisco Dominguez, Head of Latin American Studies, Middlesex University
Dr. Elizabeth Bomberg, Department of Politics, University of Edinburgh
Dr. Simon Kirby, Department of Theoretical and Applied Linguistics,
University of Edinburgh

Children at a carnival in Guadeloupe, in the Caribbean

CONTENTS

♟♟♟ Internet links ♟♟♟

Throughout this book we have recommended websites where you can find out more about people around the world. To visit the sites, go to the **Usborne Quicklinks Website**, where you will find links to all the sites.

1. Go to **www.usborne-quicklinks.com**
2. Type the keyword for this book: **peoples**
3. Type the page number of the link you want to visit.
4. Click on the links to go to the recommended sites.

The recommended websites are regularly reviewed and updated. Usborne Publishing is not responsible for the content of any website other than its own. Please read the Internet safety guidelines on page 92.

WORLD MAP

Severnaya Zemlya

New Siberia Islands

A R C T I C

O C E A N

Wrangel Island

Beaufort Sea

Victoria Island

Arctic Circle

S i b e r i a

Lena

Alaska (U.S.A.)

R U S S I A ○ Yakutsk

Anchorage ○

Yukon

C A N A

Great Plains

Yenisey

Amur

Sea of Okhotsk

Bering Sea

Vancouver ○

Ulan Bator

MONGOLIA

Gobi Desert

Beijing (Peking) ○

○ Shenyang

N. KOREA

JAPAN

Aleutian Islands

P A C I F I C

San Francisco ○

UNITED STA OF AMERI

Tianjin ○   **Seoul**

C H I N A

Plateau of Tibet

Chongqing ○   *Yangtze*

○ Shanghai

S. KOREA

Tokyo

○ Osaka

O C E A N

Los Angeles ○

Midway Islands (U.S.A.)

Tropic of Cancer

MEXICO

Mexico City

NEPAL   **BHUTAN**

Dhaka

Guangzhou (Canton) ○

Hanoi ○   ○ Hong Kong

TAIWAN

Hawaiian Islands (U.S.A.)

GUATH

SA

BANGLADESH

MYANMAR (BURMA)

Yangon (Rangoon)

Mekong

LAOS

VIETNAM

○ Manila

Northern Mariana Islands (U.S.A.)

MARSHALL ISLANDS

Bangkok

THAILAND

CAMBODIA

South China Sea

PHILIPPINES

International Date Line

Line Islands

Equator

Galapa Island (Ecuado

Kuala Lumpur ○

Putrajaya

MALAYSIA

SINGAPORE

PALAU

FEDERATED STATES OF MICRONESIA

NAURU

KIRIBATI

Sumatra

Borneo

I N D O N E S I A

New Guinea

PAPUA NEW GUINEA

SOLOMON ISLANDS

TUVALU

Marquesas Islands

Tuamotu Archipelago

Jakarta ○

Java

EAST TIMOR

Darwin ○

SAMOA

Society Islands

I N D I A N

Port Moresby

VANUATU

FRENCH POLYNESIA

Pitcairn Islands (U.K.)

Tropic of Capricorn

O C E A N

FIJI

New Caledonia (France)

TONGA

A U S T R A L I A

○ Brisbane

Perth ○

Canberra ○   ○ Sydney

P A C I F I C

○ Melbourne

NEW ZEALAND   ○ Wellington

O C E A N

Chatham Islands (New Zealand)

Antarctic Circle

Ross Sea

A N T A R

4

esmere
sland

Baffin
Bay

Baffin Island

GREENLAND
(Denmark)

Svalbard
(Norway)

North Cape

Franz Josef Land

Severnaya
Zemlya

Novaya
Zemlya

ICELAND

Reykjavik

Faroe Islands
(Denmark)

Lapland

NORWAY

SWEDEN

FINLAND

R U S S I A

Ob

Ural Mountains

Yenisey

Nuuk
(Godthåb)

A

Labrador

Newfoundland

Oslo

Helsinki

Stockholm

St. Petersburg

Moscow

**UNITED
KINGDOM**

DENMARK

ESTONIA

LATVIA

LITHUANIA

Astana

KAZAKSTAN

ntréal

wa

St. Lawrence

New York

Washington D.C.

Dublin

IRELAND

London

NETHERLANDS

RUSSIA

BELARUS

Volga

Kiev

UKRAINE

Caspian
Sea

Aral
Sea

UZBEKISTAN

Tashkent

KYRGYZSTAN

C H I N A

GERMANY

Paris

Warsaw

POLAND

Madrid Rome

Lisbon

PORTUGAL

SPAIN

ATLANTIC

Azores
(Portugal)

Madeira
(Portugal)

Rabat

Canary Islands
(Spain)

Laâyoune

WESTERN
SAHARA

CZ. REP.

FRANCE

SWITZ.

AUSTRIA HUNGARY

SLOVAKIA

SLOV.

CRO.

ITALY

BOS. &
HERZ.

YUGO.

Danube

ROMANIA

MOLDOVA

BULGARIA

MAC.

ALB.

Athens

GREECE

Black Sea

Istanbul

Ankara

TURKEY

GEORGIA

ARMENIA AZERBAIJAN

TURKMENISTAN

Ashgabat

TAJIKISTAN

Kabul

Islamabad

New
Delhi

Plateau of
Tibet

Himalaya
Mountains

NEPAL

BHUTAN

Algiers Tunis

Mediterranean Sea

CYPRUS

SYRIA

Tehran

AFGHANISTAN

PAKISTAN

Delhi

OCEAN

Bermuda
(U.K.)

MOROCCO

Atlas Mountains

TUNISIA

ISRAEL

Tripoli

Cairo

LEBANON

IRAQ

JORDAN

Baghdad

KUWAIT

IRAN

Karachi

I N D I A

Ganges

Kolkata
(Calcutta)

Dhaka

BANGLADESH

MYANMAR
(BURMA)

u

BAHAMAS

BA

DOMINICAN
REPUBLIC

HAITI

Santo Domingo

AMAICA

Caribbean

GUA Sea

ALGERIA

LIBYA

EGYPT

Nile

Red Sea

**SAUDI
ARABIA**

Riyadh

UNITED
ARAB
EMIRATES

Muscat

Arabian
Sea

Mumbai
(Bombay)

Bay
of Bengal

Yangon
(Rangoon)

THAILAND

Colombo

SRI LANKA

Sahara Desert

Nouakchott

MAURITANIA

CAPE VERDE

Dakar

SENEGAL

MALI

Bamako

NIGER

Niamey

CHAD

Khartoum

SUDAN

ERITREA

Asmara

Sana

YEMEN

OMAN

MALDIVES

Caracas

ANAMA

VENEZUELA

GUYANA

SURINAME

FRENCH
GUIANA

Amazon

COLOMBIA

otá

OR

RU

a

BURKINA
FASO

GUINEA

SIERRA
LEONE

LIBERIA

IVORY
COAST

GHANA

NIGERIA

Abuja

Lagos

Yaoundé

CAMEROON

**CENTRAL AFRICAN
REPUBLIC**

N'Djamena

Bangui

Addis Ababa

ETHIOPIA

SOMALIA

Mogadishu

SEYCHELLES

Libreville

GABON

CONGO

Brazzaville

Kinshasa

**DEMOCRATIC
REPUBLIC OF**

Congo

UGANDA

Kampala

Lake
Victoria

KENYA

Nairobi

Dodoma

BRAZIL

La Paz

BOLIVIA

Sucre

Brasília

Ascension
(U.K.)

St. Helena
(U.K.)

Luanda

ANGOLA

CONGO

TANZANIA

COMOROS

MADAGASCAR

Antananarivo

MAURITIUS

INDIAN

OCEAN

Réunion
(France)

PARAGUAY

São Paulo

Rio de Janeiro

Asunción

ZAMBIA

Lusaka

MALAWI

MOZAMBIQUE

NAMIBIA

Harare

ZIMBABWE

Windhoek

BOTSWANA

Gaborone

Maputo

Pretoria

SWAZILAND

antiago

URUGUAY

CHILE

ARGENTINA

Andes

Paraná

Buenos
Aires

Montevideo

ATLANTIC

OCEAN

**SOUTH
AFRICA**

LESOTHO

Cape Town

Cape of Good Hope

Falkland Islands
(U.K.)

South Georgia
(U.K.)

Cape Horn

South
Sandwich
Islands
(U.K.)

Kerguélen
(France)

Antarctic
Peninsula

C   T   I   C   A

WHAT ARE PEOPLE?

This book is about people and our different lifestyles, languages, religions and cultures. Humans have the most advanced culture of any species. But what are humans, and what makes us different from other animals?

A young child learns language by listening to people talk and copying them. Gradually children learn to make up their own new sentences.

The human species

Human beings are just one of millions of different kinds, or species, of animals that live on Earth. We belong to a group of animals called primates, which includes apes and monkeys. However, the way we behave is very different from all other types of animals. Humans have unusually large, complicated brains. We try to question why things happen and where we came from, and look for ways to show how we feel. This is why we are the only animals to have science and religion. We also have a complex culture, which means things like art, music, clothes and customs.

These animals are bonobos, a type of ape. They share many similarities with humans, but they are still very different from us in the way they look and behave.

Language

Humans have a much more advanced use of language than other animals. With language, we can explain ideas to each other, store information in books and computers, and pass on our knowledge to future generations.

The earliest known writing was used by the Sumerians, who lived about 5,000 years ago. Now there are hundreds of different alphabets and writing styles, which are known as scripts.

𒆳	mountain
𒊕	head
𒉿	food
𒀀	water
𒄷	bird
𒄩	fish
𒄖	ox

This Sumerian writing, called cuneiform, is one of the oldest writing systems in the world.

This woman is wearing court dress to perform a traditional Japanese tea ceremony.

Ethnic groups

This book often uses the terms "ethnic groups" and "peoples" to describe groups of people who live together, or who see themselves as a group. Ethnic groups can be large or small. They can live together or be spread over a wide area. But the people who belong to an ethnic group usually have several things in common. They may share the same language, culture or religion.

Groups of people

People are social animals. This means we like to live in groups and communicate with each other. The simplest human group is the family, a group of people linked together by birth, adoption or fostering. People also form other groups, such as bands, teams, towns, cities, political parties and whole countries.

These are dancers from Congo, in Africa, wearing costumes made from grasses. People often wear costumes or uniforms to show that they belong to a particular group.

Types of people

Wherever you go, there are differences between people. Some are taller than others. Some can run faster than others. There are people of different sexes, ages and abilities. Some people are very good at learning facts, others might be good at sports or cooking.

Sometimes, differences in appearance can help you recognize where a person might be from. But people have been moving around, or migrating, for thousands of years, so most countries have many different types of people living in them.

PEOPLES AND CULTURE

Culture means "way of life". The culture of a society or group of people includes their customs, hobbies, foods, fashions, beliefs and ways of celebrating things. Your culture depends on things like your family background, the country you live in, and your age.

Fashions, such as the clothes worn by these Japanese girls, can change very quickly.

Types of culture

Popular culture includes everyday leisure activities, fashions and media (such as TV and magazines). This type of culture changes quickly, but traditional culture is also important to most people. Religious rituals, birthday songs, and foods eaten on particular days are examples of traditional culture that stay the same from one generation to the next.

Many parts of the world, especially big cities, are multicultural. This means that they have people with many different cultures living in them. Multicultural societies often arise when groups of people migrate from one place to live in another, taking their culture with them.

Religion

Most people in the world are religious. This means they have a set of spiritual beliefs about why the world exists and what happens after death. The main religions are Buddhism, Christianity, Hinduism, Islam (whose followers are called Muslims), Judaism (whose followers are called Jews) and Sikhism.

Muslims, Christians, Jews and Sikhs believe in just one god. Hindus have many gods, who are all part of an overriding force called Brahman. Buddhism does not focus on gods, but involves following a set of rules in order to achieve a state called nirvana.

This woman from Bali, in Indonesia, is praying. Most religious people speak to their gods or spirits by praying.

♟♟♟ Internet links ♟♟♟

For links to the following websites where you can find out about countries around the world, and different peoples and their languages, customs, food and religions, go to **www.usborne-quicklinks.com**

Website 1 Find up-to-date fact files on all the world's countries.

Website 2 Travel the world and see famous sites, listen to local languages, learn basic facts, explore timelines and send virtual postcards along the way.

Website 3 Listen to the languages spoken in lots of different countries.

Website 4 Test your knowledge of table manners in countries around the world.

Website 5 Find delicious recipes and interesting food facts from many different countries.

Website 6 Discover what kinds of food children eat around the world, and why some children go hungry.

Website 7 Print out pictures from a collection of world clip art and add them to your projects.

Website 8 Find out about the festivals, beliefs and history of world religions then test your knowledge with online quizzes.

Website 9 Search a clickable calendar and learn about different religious holidays and festivals that take place every month.

Website 10 Visit the seven continents of the world and find out about endangered cultures and the animals that are important to their traditions.

Website 11 Investigate objects from different world cultures in an online museum, then try a quiz.

Making a living

Most of the people in the world have to work in order to survive and support their children. Billions of people survive by growing crops or raising animals. Some people have to move around constantly as part of their work. This is called a nomadic lifestyle. Most traditional nomads, such as the Saami of Lapland and the Tuareg of northern Africa, make a living herding animals.

As the world becomes more industrialized and modern technology develops, more and more people are working in paid jobs on big farms, in factories and mines, or in service industries such as banking and computing.

These traders are making a living by selling fresh fruit and vegetables from boats at a floating market in Thailand.

These Hagehai boys from New Guinea are learning to use bows and arrows by shooting at a flower. By the time they are eight years old, they will have to use this skill to hunt for food.

American football fans wave pom-poms at the Rose Bowl stadium, Los Angeles, California

NORTH AMERICA

NORTH AMERICA

The name "North America" is sometimes confusing, as it can be used to mean several different things. In this book, the northern part of the American continent begins with Panama in the south and stretches up to Canada and Greenland in the north. It includes the U.S.A., Mexico, Central America and the Caribbean.

This map shows where North America is.

Different lands

The landscape and climate of North America is extremely varied. Greenland and Alaska in the far north are cold, icy and sparsely populated, Arizona in the U.S.A. has vast stretches of desert, and Central America is dominated by hot, humid rainforests. Cities such as New York and Mexico City are among the biggest in the world and are filled with towering skyscrapers.

This dancer is a member of the Blackfeet group of Native Americans. He is performing at a special meeting called a powwow.

Native Americans

Native Americans are the people who lived in North America before European explorers arrived. Each Native American group had its own lifestyles and customs and was governed by a chief.

In the 19th century, the European settlers forced Native Americans to live on areas of land called reservations. They tried to force them to speak English, wear European clothes and become Christians. As a result, many Native American languages and traditions were forgotten. Now languages are being revived and Native Americans make and sell traditional pottery, baskets or textiles. Some groups also run casinos on their reservations.

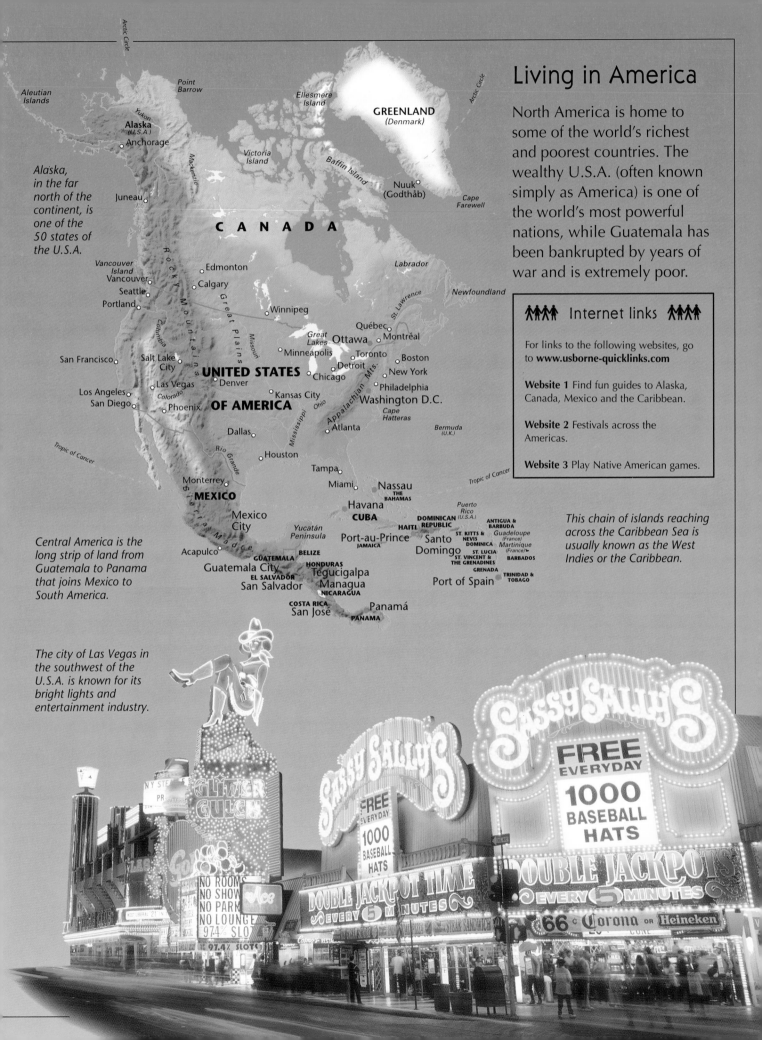

Living in America

North America is home to some of the world's richest and poorest countries. The wealthy U.S.A. (often known simply as America) is one of the world's most powerful nations, while Guatemala has been bankrupted by years of war and is extremely poor.

👪 Internet links 👪

For links to the following websites, go to **www.usborne-quicklinks.com**

Website 1 Find fun guides to Alaska, Canada, Mexico and the Caribbean.

Website 2 Festivals across the Americas.

Website 3 Play Native American games.

Alaska, in the far north of the continent, is one of the 50 states of the U.S.A.

Central America is the long strip of land from Guatemala to Panama that joins Mexico to South America.

This chain of islands reaching across the Caribbean Sea is usually known as the West Indies or the Caribbean.

The city of Las Vegas in the southwest of the U.S.A. is known for its bright lights and entertainment industry.

THE U.S.A.

The United States of America, also known as the U.S.A. or America, is a huge country, although it's not much more than half the size of Russia, the biggest country. The U.S.A. is very rich and has immense political and cultural influence worldwide.

Land and law

The U.S.A. is divided into 50 states. Power is shared between state governments and a central federal government based in the capital, Washington D.C. The southern states are warm, green and rich in oil, while the main farming areas are in the western states. The northeast is the main business region. Manufacturing has moved more to the southern states in recent years. Many computer companies are located in Silicon Valley in California.

The U.S.A. has hundreds of large theme parks with huge rides like this roller coaster.

The 'American Dream'

People from all over the world have moved to the U.S.A., and a million new immigrants arrive each year. Many are following the 'American Dream': the belief that, in America, anyone can become rich and successful. However, many Americans are still very poor.

The mixture of peoples gives the U.S.A. a rich, diverse culture. Jazz and blues music, for instance, developed out of rhythms brought to the U.S.A. from Africa, while cheesecake and bagels were originally Jewish foods.

Dr. Martin Luther King Jr., the leader of the 1960s Civil Rights movement for equality for black Americans, speaks at a "March against Fear" rally in 1966.

The crowned figure in the background is the Statue of Liberty in New York. It is a symbol of the political freedom enshrined in the Constitution of the U.S.A.

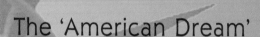 Internet links

For links to the following websites, go to **www.usborne-quicklinks.com**

Website 1 Watch video clips and listen to songs from America's past.

Website 2 Find out how Americans celebrate the anniversary of their independence.

Website 3 Learn about the history and structure of the U.S.A. Government.

Website 4 Watch a slide show of the latest Shuttle launch.

Entertainment

Entertainment is big business in the U.S.A. The country's main movie-making area, Hollywood, in California, produces films that can cost many millions of dollars to make, but which earn even more. Theme parks are also very popular.

Science and power

The U.S.A. is the leading political world power, and science and technology have played an important part in its success. Nuclear science, which can be used to make powerful bombs, has helped give the U.S.A. political strength. As a result, the U.S.A. now plays a big part in making wars and keeping peace around the world. The nation's wealth and success also owe a lot to computer science, and the U.S.A. dominates Internet technology. American English is the main language of the Internet.

Minnie Mouse posing for a photo with a young boy in Disney World, a theme park based on famous characters from the cartoons of Walt Disney

The reusable Space Shuttle spacecraft is part of America's world-famous multi-billion dollar space exploration industry.

THE FAR NORTH

In Canada, people ski in resorts where there are ski lifts and other facilities, but people also ski cross country just to get from place to place.

The far north of North America is taken up by Greenland, Canada and Alaska (part of the U.S.A.). This is a vast area: Canada is the second largest country in the world, and Greenland is the world's biggest island.

Many cultures

Canada is divided into ten provinces and three territories: the Yukon, Nunavut and the Northwest Territories.

Many Canadians have British, French or Native American ancestors and the offical languages are English and French. French culture is strong in the province of Québec where cafes and shops reflect its influence.

Skiers swoop down a slope at the Lake Louise Ski Area in Banff National Park, Alberta, Canada. Many tourists visit Canada for its natural beauty and outdoor activities.

Natural resources

Most Canadians live in large cities along the border with the U.S.A. The rest of the country has a varied landscape, including lakes, mountains, forests and grasslands, or prairies. These provide rich natural resources such as timber, water, gas, oil and minerals. Outside the cities, many people's jobs are based around mining and forestry.

Winter sports

Outdoor sports and activities such as canoeing, riding horses and rafting are popular in Canada. But the country is particularly known for its winter sports, especially ice hockey which can be played on frozen ponds and lakes.

Snowmobiling at a winter sports festival in Canada

Greenland

Although Greenland is the world's largest island, its population is very small because conditions there are so harsh. Most of Greenland lies within the Arctic Circle, and its central region is covered by a layer of ice that never melts.

The island has a small road network, but planes and dog sleds provide a flexible and reliable way of getting around. The majority of Greenlanders live along the coast, where the climate is mildest, making a living from catching fish, shrimps and seals.

Villages in Greenland are small. This one has about 500 human residents and 2,000 sled dogs, which are used for hunting and transportation.

These Inuit people are wearing heavy animal-skin coats to keep warm.

♟♟♟♟ Internet links ♟♟♟♟

For links to the following websites, go to **www.usborne-quicklinks.com**

Website 1 Go on an Arctic adventure and explore Nunavut.

Website 2 Play games to find out more about Canada.

Website 3 Meet schoolchildren who live in Canada.

Who are the Inuit?

The Inuit are the native people of northern Canada. In 1999, the Canadian government made part of the Northwest Territories into a new Inuit territory, giving back land which the Inuit had lost to settlers. The new territory is called Nunavut, which means "our land" in Inukitut, the Inuit language.

The Inuit keep their traditions alive by speaking Inukitut, hunting for food, and making wood and bone carvings. They also take advantage of modern technology, using snowmobiles, telephones and computers.

MEXICO

Mexico is a big country between the U.S.A. and Central America. It is very mountainous, but most Mexicans live in towns and cities in the middle of the country, where the land is flat.

A reconstruction of the Aztec calendar, on display in the National Museum of Anthropology in Mexico City

The Aztecs

From the mid-14th century, Mexico was ruled by the Aztecs, a Native American people. They built an empire with a capital city called Tenochtitlan and ruled over many Native American peoples. The empire ended when the Spanish conquered Mexico in 1519. Today's Mexicans are mainly *mestizos*, of mixed Spanish and Native American descent.

Hot and spicy

Mexican food is popular all over the world. *Guacamole* (mashed avocados), *tortillas* (flat bread), and meat and beans cooked in tomato sauce with hot chillies* are typical Mexican dishes. Over 60 different kinds of chillies are grown in Mexico. In some areas, people eat salads made out of cactus plants.

Corn tortilla chips are eaten with Mexican-style dips around the world.

Mexico City

Mexico City, the capital of Mexico, was built directly over the ruins of the Aztec capital. Today it is the world's biggest city, with 22 million people. The majority of the country's business is there, and the city is extremely busy, with lots of noise and traffic. It lies in a valley overlooked by volcanoes, and is regularly affected by earthquakes. The soil beneath it is so soft and swampy that the city sinks a little each year.

Tomatoes, chillies and beans are key ingredients in many Mexican dishes.*

*Chilies (U.S.A.)

Day of the Dead

The Day of the Dead is a joyous celebration that takes place on November 2 each year. All over Mexico, markets and shops sell skeletons and skulls made out of sugar or bread. People also dress up as skeletons and dance in huge parades. At home, families make small altars which they use to pray for and remember their dead friends and relatives. They decorate the altars with flowers, candles, food and photographs of those they want to remember.

👨‍👩‍👧 Internet links 👨‍👩‍👧

For links to the following websites, go to **www.usborne-quicklinks.com**

Website 1 "Day of the Dead" photos, facts and recipes.

Website 2 Meet a Mexican family and find out about life in Mexico.

Website 3 Find out more about the Aztecs.

This skeleton model has been made from papier-mâché for a Day of the Dead parade.

CENTRAL AMERICA

These girls are dressed as angels to take part in a religious procession in El Salvador. Religious festivals are common in Central America.

Central America is the narrow strip of land, or isthmus, connecting North and South America. The landscape of Central America is mainly made up of mountains and volcanoes and people's lives are affected by frequent earthquakes and volcanic eruptions.

Takeover

Like Mexico, Central America was conquered by the Spanish 500 years ago, and many people living there today are of mixed Spanish and Native American descent. But each country has its own mix of peoples. As well as Native Americans and people of European descent, there are people of African descent along the Caribbean coast.

Land of the Maya

The Maya had a powerful empire around AD200-900, when they built great cities. Their empire covered most of Guatemala, and parts of Belize, Mexico, Honduras and El Salvador. Ruined cities can still be found in the jungles of Guatemala. The Maya are no longer powerful, but they still make up nearly half of Guatemala's population.

This Mayan girl in Guatemala is carrying a younger child on her back, wrapped in a traditional Mayan shawl.

♟ Internet links ♟

For links to the following websites, go to **www.usborne-quicklinks.com**

Website 1 Learn about Mayan people by examining their textiles.

Website 2 Watch animations of how the Panama Canal works.

The Soccer War

Central America has suffered from decades of civil wars and conflict between countries. One war broke out between El Salvador and Honduras in 1969, after they had played soccer against each other in the World Cup. The real reasons, however, were disagreements over land, trade, and Salvadorean refugees in Honduras.

Worry dolls

Children in Central America sometimes make tiny, bright dolls called worry dolls. There is a legend that if they tell the dolls their worries at night and then place them under their pillows, by morning all their worries will have disappeared.

These tiny dolls are worry dolls. Their clothes are made by wrapping thread around the bodies.

The Panama Canal

The Panama Canal is one of the most important waterways in the world. It is a channel of water 80km (50 miles) long that cuts through Panama, linking the Atlantic Ocean with the Pacific Ocean. Each vessel that uses the canal must pay a fee according to its weight. This means that while ships pay thousands of dollars, Richard Halliburton, who swam through the canal in 1928, only paid 36 cents.

A thatched bohio, or hut, in a rainforest clearing in Panama. Huts like these are the homes of the Guaymi people, who live on the border between Panama and Costa Rica.

Rainforest life

A large area of Central America is covered by rainforest, which is home to a huge variety of plants and animals. But the rainforest is being devastated and many plants and animals may die out as trees are cut down to make timber for export, and to clear land for farming.

A rich variety of fruit is grown on the tropical islands of the Caribbean.

Pineapple

THE CARIBBEAN

The Caribbean is the name given to the chain of hundreds of tropical islands stretching from North America to South America across the Caribbean Sea.

Slavery

From around 1500, Europeans fought with each other over possession of the Caribbean islands. They brought slaves from Africa, the Middle East, the Far East, and India to work on sugar, tobacco and cocoa plantations. Many of today's inhabitants are descendants of these slaves. Languages from around the world have combined to form unique regional dialects known as *creoles*.

Mango

Papaya

Plantains are green fruits which belong to the same family as bananas.

Tourism

The Caribbean islands are known for their white sandy beaches, clear blue sea and tropical sunshine. Their beauty and isolation has given them a reputation of being a "paradise on earth". As a result, tourism is one of the Caribbean's most important industries.

Tourists often go diving in the clear blue sea of the Caribbean. This boy is looking at a shell he has found while diving at Virgin Gorda, in the British Virgin Islands.

Hard work

Although the Caribbean may be seen as a paradise by people who go there as tourists, life is not always easy for its inhabitants. Many of those who do not work in the tourist industry make a living growing sugar cane, the Caribbean's main export, and other crops such as bananas, coffee and tobacco. Some of the poorest states, such as Haiti, suffer from severe unemployment. Many Haitians have to cross the border into the wealthier Dominican Republic to find work.

Music

Africa has had an important influence on the music of the Caribbean. Many Caribbean musical styles, such as reggae, conga, cha-cha-cha, plena and calypso, have African roots. Calypso, which originated in Trinidad is the music style most associated with the Caribbean. Calypso songs are often improvised and tend to focus on social and political subjects.

Street parties

Carnivals held to mark religious festivals are an important part of island life. The main carnival season takes place before Lent (the period of 40 days leading up to Easter in the Christian calendar). The streets are filled with parades, loud music, and people singing and dancing in bright costumes.

Junkanoo is a huge festival in the Bahamas. People make flamboyant costumes like this to take part in parades.

A busy outdoor market in Zumbahua, Ecuador

SOUTH AMERICA

SOUTH AMERICA

T he people of South America have a huge range of cultures and backgrounds. Over the centuries, waves of settlers have arrived from Europe, Africa and Asia to join the Native Americans who have lived there for thousands of years.

This map shows where South America is.

Empty and crowded

Much of South America is covered in rainforest, mountains and deserts where it can be hard to survive. Many people live in small villages and most work as farmers. Yet the coast has some of the world's biggest cities, with towering skyscrapers and crowded shanty towns.

Caracas

VENEZUELA

Medellín

Bogotá

Orinoco

Georgetown
Paramaribo
Cayenne

Cali

GUYANA
SURINAME
FRENCH GUIANA

COLOMBIA

Guiana Highlands

Equator

Equator

Belém

Quito

ECUADOR

Galapagos Islands (Ecuador)

Manaus

Fortaleza

Amazon

S e l v a s

Recife

B R A Z I L

PERU

Lima

M a t o

G r o s s o

São Francisco

Salvador

Brasília

Lake Titicaca

La Paz

BOLIVIA
Sucre

Brazilian Highlands

Belo Horizonte

Atacama Desert

Rio de Janeiro

PARAGUAY

São Paulo

Tropic of Capricorn

Asunción

Curitiba

Paraná

Porto Alegre

Córdoba

Rosario

URUGUAY

Santiago

C H I L E

Andes

A R G E N T I N A

Pampas

Buenos Aires

Montevideo

Patagonia

Falkland Islands (U.K.)

Tierra del Fuego

Cape Horn

Native Americans

Experts think the first South Americans came from Asia. They probably walked across a narrow strip of land in the far north, which once joined what are now Russia and Alaska. Their descendents now live mostly in South America's mountainous countries, such as Colombia, Bolivia, Ecuador and Peru.

Catholic continent

Although there are many different types of people in South America, over 90% of them are Roman Catholics. This form of Christianity was introduced by Spanish and Portuguese invaders who took control of the continent in the 1500s. There are now Catholic churches and statues all over South America, and many Christian festivals are celebrated.

Other religions

Many South Americans worship traditional Native American or African gods and spirits, often as well as attending a Catholic church. Some of the traditional religions have priests called shamans, who are believed to have magical powers.

Latin languages

South America is sometimes called Latin America, because most South Americans speak the Latin-based languages Spanish and Portuguese. These were brought by European invaders in the 16th century. However, many people speak Native American languages, such as Quechua and Aymara.

This crowded beach is the famous Copacabana beach in Rio de Janeiro, Brazil.

♦♦♦♦ Internet links ♦♦♦♦

For links to the following websites, go to
www.usborne-quicklinks.com

Website 1 Visit South American countries.

Website 2 Meet a family in Peru and learn about weaving in the Andes.

Website 3 Fascinating facts about the ancient Americas.

A shaman collects bark from a rainforest tree to use in traditional medicines.

IN THE MOUNTAINS

The vast Andes mountain range snakes down the western side of South America, through Colombia, Ecuador, Peru, Bolivia, Chile and Argentina. Despite dangers from volcanoes and earthquakes, the Andes are home to millions of miners, farmers, craftspeople and city-dwellers.

This young boy from Ecuador is harnessing a llama to lead it to market.

Fertile farms

The peaks of the Andes are covered in snow, but the lower slopes are good for growing crops. Mountain farmers grow corn, coffee and other crops on small plots of land, sometimes with terraces to stop the soil from being washed away. If the land is not good enough for crops, they keep herds of mountain animals, such as llamas and alpacas, which provide milk and wool, and which may also be used to transport goods.

Craft work

Many Native Americans live in villages in the Andes. Some earn a living from traditional crafts. They weave brightly striped shawls, blankets and hats. These are used by local people as well as being sold to tourists and exported around the world.

A traditional mountain folk band playing for tourists in Machu Picchu, Peru

Mountain music

The traditional folk music of the Andes combines Native American and Spanish sounds. It is usually played outside in the street or at folk clubs called *peñas*. When musicians play for tourists, they often wear traditional dress.

This is a view over La Paz, Bolivia. At over 3,650m (12,000ft), it is the world's highest capital city.

Cities

The Andes has some large cities, including Colombia's capital, Bogotá, and La Paz, one of Bolivia's two capitals (the other is Sucre). Most city-dwellers work in factories or mines. In the mountains there are huge deposits of gold, copper, tin, coal and jewels, especially emeralds. The biggest emerald mines are in Muzo, Colombia. While mine workers use modern machinery to extract the emeralds, poor *Guaqueros* (or "treasure hunters") sift through the dust and rubble, hoping to find leftover gems.

Inca influence

The Tahuantinsuyo, also known as the Incas, once ruled a large area of western South America. Their reign ended 400 years ago, but they still influence the Andean countries today.

Quechua, the Inca language, is spoken by about 13 million people. Mountain farmers use terraces that were built by the Incas, and ruined Inca cities, such as Machu Picchu in Peru, are tourist attractions.

This Peruvian girl in traditional costume is one of the Quechua people, who are descended from the Incas.

RAINFOREST PEOPLES

South America's huge Amazon valley is covered in millions of square miles of thick, humid rainforest. The Amazon rainforest is so big that it contains over a third of the world's trees. For thousands of years, it has also been the home of Native American peoples.

Leaders of the Kayapo people of Brazil sometimes wear lip-plates like these which emphasise their roles as public speakers.

Traditional lives

The rainforest is so vast that groups of people living in it have been cut off from the rest of the world for centuries. Some have only recently been discovered by outsiders. There may be others who have never had contact with the outside world. Rainforest peoples such as the Jivaro, Txikao and Kayapo have their own languages and customs. But many of them share similar lifestyles, surviving by hunting animals, gathering fruits and nuts, and growing crops in forest clearings.

Losing lifestyles

As new roads are built into the rainforest, the people who live there have more contact with outsiders. They may even lose their homes when parts of the rainforest are cut down. To make a living, they may have to learn more widely spoken languages or move away from the forest into towns and cities, leaving their old traditions and lifestyles behind.

👬👬👬 Internet links 👬👬👬

For links to the following websites, go to **www.usborne-quicklinks.com**

Website 1 Watch a slide show about people who live in the rainforest.

Websites 2 and 3 Run an ecotourism project in the Amazon and join an expedition to the Amazon.

This man playing a wooden flute is one of the Jivaro people of the Amazon.

Clearing the forest

Rainforest trees provide all kinds of useful products, such as brazil nuts, cashew nuts, wax and rubber. At one time these things were simply collected from the forest, but now they are mostly farmed on plantations.

Traditionally, rainforest peoples cleared small areas of land to grow crops, and moved on after a few years. Because the cleared areas were tiny, this method, called shifting agriculture, did not harm much of the forest, and the trees eventually grew back. But since the 1960s, more rainforest has been cut down, for timber and to make space for farms, mines and factories. So the amount of rainforest is decreasing.

These are rainforest plants in Ecuador. Many rainforest plants can be used to make medicines.

Forest food

Although most rainforest peoples grow crops, they can also find food in the forest. Hunting and fishing provide them with a wide range of meat, including monkeys, toucans and caimans, which are reptiles similar to alligators. The Piaroa people of Venezuela sometimes eat tarantulas (a type of spider), cooking them by squeezing their insides onto a leaf and baking it over a fire.

Many rainforest peoples grow just enough food to supply their village. This woman is processing locally-grown manioc (a plant a little like a potato) to make flour.

COMBINED CULTURES

South American culture is influenced by the traditions of the different types of people who live there. For example, many South Americans love soccer, which came from Europe; samba music from Africa; and foods that combine Spanish, African and Native American influences.

Party!

Carnivals and costume parades take place frequently all over South America. Most of them celebrate Christian festivals, such as Lent, Easter and Christmas. They are lively occasions, with plenty of loud music, dancing, dressing up, eating and drinking. Many cities, towns and villages also hold their own local religious or historical celebrations.

These costumed dancers are taking part in a parade in Venezuela, held to mark the Catholic feast of Corpus Christi.

Delicious dishes

All kinds of foods are eaten in South America. Argentinians and Uruguayans eat lots of meat, and Bolivians have dozens of varieties of potatoes. A typical meal in the Andes consists of fried beef, beans, a fried egg, rice and a slice of avocado. This type of dish is called *churrasco* in Ecuador and *bandeja paisa* in Colombia. Local delicacies include *cuy* (guinea pig) and *hormiga culona* (fried ants) in Colombia, and iguana (a type of lizard) in Guyana.

This Peruvian woman is preparing guinea pigs for roasting.

Soccer fever

Soccer is the biggest sport in South America, and national team members are heroes. Uruguay hosted and won the first ever soccer World Cup in 1930. Since then Argentina has won twice and Brazil has won four times, making it the only country ever to do so. Children play soccer in the streets all over South America. Most towns and villages have local teams, and even rainforest-dwellers have a patch of land set aside for soccer games.

𝝠𝝠𝝠𝝠 Internet links 𝝠𝝠𝝠𝝠

For links to websites where you can discover some of the shared history and traditions of the people of South America and listen to music from different regions, go to **www.usborne-quicklinks.com**

These children are playing informal games of soccer by an old fort at Sacsahuaman, near Cuzco in Peru.

African influence

Culture along the east coast of South America has a strong African element. People from West Africa arrived as slaves hundreds of years ago, to work in mines and on sugar plantations for the area's European rulers. Their beliefs, music and culture had an important influence, which is still present today. African rhythms blended with Spanish, Portuguese and Native American sounds to produce musical styles such as samba and salsa. Many Brazilians follow a spiritual religion called Candomblé, which is based on African traditions.

This dancer represents the God of Medicine in the Candomblé religion.

BRAZIL

Brazil is the biggest country in South America. It contains most of the Amazon rainforest and also has some of the world's largest cities. In many ways it is a very modern country, with futuristic buildings and high-tech industries, but a lot of its people are still poor.

This 30m (100ft) high statue of Christ stands on Corcovado Hill above Rio de Janeiro. Its shape can be seen from far out at sea.

Portugal and Brazil

Unlike the rest of South America, Brazil was once ruled by Portugal, and its main language is Portuguese. This happened because just before 1500, news reached Europe that the Spanish had discovered lands not previously known to Europeans, which they called the "New World". Portugal wanted some of the land for itself, so the two countries agreed that Portugal could take over the eastern side of the continent. Brazil has been independent from Portugal since 1822.

Carnaval

Brazil is famous for its festivals, music and nightclubs. The most famous event is Carnaval (the Brazilian spelling of "carnival"). Carnaval celebrations are held all over Brazil every February or March, to mark the start of Lent.

The celebrations go on for five days, with feasting, dancing, a huge costume parade and samba competitions. Samba is a type of percussion music popular in Brazil. There are special samba schools where people can learn samba music and dancing.

A samba dancer twirls at Rio's famous Carnaval.

A new capital

In 1956 the Brazilian government began to build a new capital city, Brasília. Brasília was planned as a modern, hi-tech city and it is still known for its space-age buildings. It was designed to be fast and easy to drive around, so it had no traffic lights. But when people moved in, they complained that it was too hard to cross the roads, so the design was changed.

👨‍👩‍👧 Internet links 👨‍👩‍👧

For links to websites where you can take a fun journey through Brazil and find out more about the people, music and food, and the fast-growing cities, go to **www.usborne-quicklinks.com**

Cities out of control

The populations of many of Brazil's cities, such as São Paulo and Rio de Janeiro, are rising fast as more and more people from rural areas arrive, looking for jobs and homes.

Often there is not enough housing for the new arrivals, and so shanty towns develop on the outskirts of cities. These are made up of makeshift houses built out of scrap metal and junk. The shanty towns are nicknamed *favelas* after a type of hillside flower.

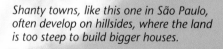

Shanty towns, like this one in São Paulo, often develop on hillsides, where the land is too steep to build bigger houses.

This is the Metropolitan Cathedral in Brasília. It is a good example of the city's modern architecture.

Masked partygoers at the Venice Carnival in Italy

EUROPE

EUROPE

Although Europe is the second smallest continent in the world, it contains over 40 countries, and its peoples speak more than 50 different languages. Throughout history there have been many migrations* within, to and from Europe.

This map shows where Europe is.

Ancient Europe

For nearly six centuries, until around AD500, the Romans ruled much of Europe. Today, there are similarities in law, language, architecture and education across the continent that date back to the Romans. The Romans took many of their ideas from the Greeks, who had their own powerful empire and culture.

Christianity

Christianity has been the main religion in Europe since the days of the Roman Empire. Today, many Europeans do not go to church regularly, and many others follow different religions. Yet the influence of Christianity on art, architecture and culture can be seen all over Europe.

European arts

Europe has produced many great artists, composers and writers. The ancient Greek poet Homer and the English playwright Shakespeare, composers like Bach, Mozart and Beethoven, and artists such as Michelangelo and Picasso are famous around the world. Europe also attracts millions of tourists every year to see its ancient ruins, beautiful architecture and fine art galleries.

Art exhibitions, concerts, plays and other performances are an important part of European culture. These are performers in an opera at the Royal Opera House, London.

The peninsula which includes Norway, Sweden, Finland and Denmark is known as Scandinavia.

North Cape

Arctic Circle

Lapland

Kola Peninsula

The Ural Mountains mark the eastern border of Europe.

Reykjavik
ICELAND

Arctic Circle

Faroe Islands
(Denmark)

NORWAY

SWEDEN

FINLAND

Just a fraction of Russia is in Europe, but the majority of Russians live in the European part of their country.

Oslo

Helsinki

St. Petersburg

R U S S I A

Stockholm

Tallinn
ESTONIA

Moscow

Riga
LATVIA

UNITED KINGDOM

Dublin
IRELAND

DENMARK

Copenhagen

LITHUANIA
Vilnius
RUSSIA

Minsk

BELARUS

Volgograd

London

Amsterdam

NETHERLANDS

Berlin

Warsaw

Dnieper

Kiev

Volga

Brussels

GERMANY

POLAND

BELGIUM

LUXEMBOURG

Prague

Kraków

U K R A I N E

Paris

Seine

Rhine

CZECH REPUBLIC

Carpathians

SLOVAKIA

Vienna

Bratislava

MOLDOVA

Chisinau

LIECHTENSTEIN

Budapest

FRANCE

Berne

AUSTRIA

HUNGARY

SWITZERLAND

SLOVENIA

Ljubljana

Zagreb

ROMANIA

CROATIA

Belgrade

Bucharest

Milan

SAN MARINO

BOSNIA & HERZEGOVINA

Danube

The Caucasus Mountains in Georgia and Russia provide another of Europe's natural borders.

Pyrenees

Marseille

MONACO

Sarajevo

SERBIA & MONTENEGRO

Sofia

Caucasus

PORTUGAL

ANDORRA

Tagus

Madrid

Barcelona

Corsica

Rome

ITALY

Apennines

Tirana

Skopje

BULGARIA

MACEDONIA

Istanbul

TURKEY

sbon

SPAIN

Balearic Islands

Sardinia

ALBANIA

Only the northwestern tip of Turkey is in Europe. The Turkish city of Istanbul lies half in Europe and half in Asia.

The Mediterranean coast is a popular tourist destination for Europeans.

Sicily

GREECE

Athens

MALTA

Crete

Europe divided

After the Second World War, much of eastern Europe was under the control of the Communist U.S.S.R.* Political differences between the U.S.S.R. and the non-Communist west increased until Europe split in two. The term "Iron Curtain" was used to describe the divide. In 1961, East German authorities erected a wall in the German city of Berlin to prevent people fleeing from east to west. The wall was guarded by armed soldiers. In 1989, protests against the lack of freedom led to the destruction of the Berlin Wall.

*Migrations, 7; U.S.S.R., 70

WESTERN EUROPE

Pasta is popular around the world, but originally it came from Italy. Here are some of the different pasta shapes.

In western Europe, most people live in cities or towns. City life can be fast and exciting and most western European cities have lots of stores, restaurants, cinemas, concert halls and museums. But many cities are also crowded and polluted.

Food culture

The food of western Europe is extremely varied and many countries are known for particular foods or ways of eating. For example, Italy is known for pizzas and pasta, Germany for sausages, Greece for kebabs and France for breads and cheeses. Many Spanish bars serve small snacks called tapas with drinks. These foods are popular in other countries around the world too.

Work in industry

Many western Europeans have jobs in industry, designing and making products such as cars and clothes. As more factories use machines and computers to make their products, more people are getting jobs in service industries. These are jobs which involve doing things for other people. Hotel staff, bank managers and TV presenters are examples of service jobs.

Rural life

In a few parts of western Europe, farmers still use oxen to pull farm machinery, and harvest their crops by hand. But in most areas, only large, industrialized modern farms can survive, so smaller farms are disappearing.

The Mediterranean

The northern coast of the Mediterranean Sea forms the southern border of Europe. People who live there enjoy long, hot, dry summers, which make the Mediterranean area a popular tourist destination. Many of the people living around the coast work in the tourist industry.

ᛉᛘᛘᛘ Internet links ᛘᛘᛘᛉ

For links to the following websites, go to **www.usborne-quicklinks.com**

Website 1 Try some traditional European recipes.

Website 2 View photo galleries of Venice and watch a video clip of a carnival.

Website 3 Take virtual tours of three European countries, the UK, France and Spain.

Website 4 Watch some video clips about a cheese rolling festival, a traditional event which is held every year in Gloucestershire, England.

These are small ornamental masks sold as souvenirs in Venice. Full-size masks like these are worn by "masqueraders" at Venice's annual carnival.

A watery city

Western Europe has many impressive historical cities, but one of the most unusual is Venice in Italy, which is divided into more than a hundred tiny islands by a network of canals. There are no cars there, so people get around on foot or by boat. There are special "bus" boats that provide public transport and long, narrow boats called gondolas which tourists take short rides in.

The Arc de Triomphe in Paris, France's capital, is a war monument which was commissioned by Napoleon in 1806. Today it is surrounded by huge, traffic-filled roads.

Unusual festivals

Western Europeans celebrate many festivals including religious and national holidays, but there are also many unusual regional celebrations. For example, near Gloucester, England, there is a competition where people chase cheeses down a hill.

A dancer in Madrid, Spain, performs a traditional flamenco dance, involving dramatic stamping and twirling movements.

At the Sylvesterchlausen new year celebration in Urnäsch, Switzerland, people wearing masks go from house to house ringing bells and dancing.

Spain has lots of local festivals. In Buñol, there is a huge annual tomato fight, and in Catalonia people make human castles by standing on one another's shoulders. Pamplona has a festival where people run through the streets ahead of bulls.

EASTERN EUROPE

Until the 1990s much of eastern Europe was ruled by the former Communist power the U.S.S.R.* But in the late 1980s and the 1990s, people rebelled against their Communist leaders, and today the area is a patchwork of independent states.

This is a corridor in a school near Chernobyl which was evacuated after a nuclear disaster.

Peoples at war

Over the centuries, eastern Europe has seen many wars. In recent years, fighting broke out when small ethnic groups demanded more freedom from the people who ruled over them. For example, Yugoslavia, now called Serbia and Montenegro, was once much bigger. It contained many peoples: Serbs, Bosnians, Croats, Slovenes, Montenegrins, Albanians and Macedonians. Since the Communist collapse in 1990, wars have raged in the area as ethnic groups have fought to set up their own states.

Pollution

Pollution is a big problem in eastern Europe. Many factories, set up under Communism, still use old-fashioned fuels and methods which allow toxic gases to escape. In 1986, an accident at a nuclear power station at Chernobyl, in Ukraine, sent radioactive dust into the air, polluting large areas of Europe. Hundreds of people had to leave their villages and the radiation made many people ill.

Trade links

The collapse of the U.S.S.R. and Communism has led to an explosion of trade between eastern Europe and the rest of the world. As well as selling products such as wine and factory goods, eastern European countries have become major buyers of new technology such as computing systems and mobile phones.

This is a statue from Statue Park, in Hungary. The park contains Communist statues that once stood in public places.

*Communism, U.S.S.R., 70

Spa towns

Spas are springs containing minerals. During the nineteenth century, it became fashionable throughout Europe to drink and bathe in spa waters. Many resorts were developed to cater for visitors. There are numerous spas throughout eastern Europe which remain popular today, such as those in Budapest in Hungary, and Karlovy Vary and Mariánské Lázně in the Czech Republic. People can still go to these places to drink the waters.

☗☗☗☗ Internet links ☗☗☗☗

For links to the following websites, go to
www.usborne-quicklinks.com

Website 1 Take a photo tour of Prague's buildings, including the "Ginger and Fred".

Website 2 Find out about the countries of Croatia and Slovenia, which were once part of Yugoslavia.

Website 3 Discover the real Romanian story behind the legend of Count Dracula.

Old age record

Georgia has more people who live to be over 100 than any other country. Many Georgians suggest this is due to their outdoor lifestyle, gentle climate and fertile farmland. According to Georgian legend, when God created the Georgians, he didn't have any land left for them to live on. So he had to give them the piece of land he had saved for himself, which was the best in the world.

Architecture

Many cities of eastern Europe, such as Prague, Kraków and Budapest, have well-preserved old towns. These have winding cobbled streets and a wide variety of architecture, including impressive churches and castles. Some houses are made from wood and many larger houses have distinctive painted facades, or fronts. However, some cities, such as Warsaw in Poland, which had to be heavily rebuilt after the Second World War, are dominated by modern apartment buildings.

This modern building in Prague was designed by an architect named Frank Gehry. It is nicknamed "Ginger and Fred" after the dancers Ginger Rogers and Fred Astaire, because its shape looks a little like a dancing couple.

NORTHERN EUROPE

Denmark, Sweden, Norway and Finland form the area known as Scandinavia. Together with the volcanic island of Iceland, they make up northern Europe. There is very little poverty in Scandinavia and Iceland, and their clean cities and countryside are envied by many.

People bathing in the Blue Lagoon, a warm spring near Keflavik in Iceland

Land of the Midnight Sun

The northern part of Scandinavia juts far into the Arctic Circle, the area around the North Pole. In midwinter, for about a month, the people who live there see no daylight at all, while from the end of May until the end of July the sun never sets. Because of this, it is sometimes known as the Land of the Midnight Sun.

This hotel in Sweden is made entirely of ice. Every summer it melts and has to be rebuilt the following winter. Even the glasses people drink from are made of ice.

Skiing is a popular leisure activity in Scandinavia. In winter, it's also a way of getting to and from school and work.

Winter months

During the winter, much of northern Europe is covered in snow. In many places, skiing becomes the easiest way of getting around. Children often learn to ski as soon as they can walk, and some ski to school every morning. Many places hold annual ski competitions.

The environment

Many children and adults in Scandinavia belong to 'green' groups that try to protect the environment by looking after the countryside and preventing pollution. Governments run recycling projects to collect reusable products from people's homes, and Scandinavia leads the way in building eco-friendly homes which use solar panels and insulation to save energy.

Lapland

Lapland, in the far north of Scandinavia, is one of the last areas of wilderness in Europe. It stretches from northern Russia across the north of Finland, and through parts of Sweden and Norway. It is home to the Saami, a people with their own language and culture. Some of the Saami still live a traditional lifestyle and herd reindeer. Their traditional homes are conical tents called *kota*. But these days most Saami live in houses, grouped together in small villages.

♦♦♦♦ Internet links ♦♦♦♦

For links to the following websites, go to www.usborne-quicklinks.com

Website 1 Explore an ice hotel.

Website 2 Go sightseeing in Iceland and find facts about Scandinavia.

Website 3 Watch a slide show about the Sami people.

A Saami reindeer herder in northern Norway tends a newborn reindeer calf.

Daring design

Scandinavia is famous for its exciting design styles. Scandinavian companies are renowned for making everyday objects, like chairs, tables and cars, that are simple to use yet beautiful to look at. The Scandinavian style is now copied all over the world.

A UNITING EUROPE

Most of Europe's countries belong to organizations such as the European Union and the Council of Europe, in which several states band together to support each other. Many Europeans feel this has major advantages, although others worry that countries may lose their individuality.

Representatives of E.U. states meet in Strasbourg, France.

What is the E.U.?

The E.U., or European Union, is the most important European organization. It dates from 1957, when Belgium, France, Italy, Germany, Luxembourg and the Netherlands formed the E.E.C. (European Economic Community) to improve trade and cooperation between their countries. The group changed over the years, and in 1993 it became known as the European Union. By the year 2000 it had 15 members, with more applying to join.

Free trade

The E.U. has set up laws to allow its member states to trade with each other easily. The E.U. also has laws to regulate measuring systems and safety standards for its workers, and workers from any E.U. state can work in any other without a visa or work permit.

👫👫 Internet links 👫👫

For links to the following websites, go to **www.usborne-quicklinks.com**

Website 1 A short guide to the EU with an animation showing how the EU has grown.

Website 2 Key facts and figures about the EU.

Website 3 Take a fun look at the Euro and find out which countries use this currency.

The E.U. flag and the flags of its member states. Can you identify which country each flag belongs to?

Single currency

In the 1990s, the European Union began to introduce a single currency called the Euro. Eventually it is intended to replace the national currencies of all the member states. However, some countries did not join the single currency immediately. It was launched on January 1, 1999, with 11 member states taking part.

These are 50-cent coins, part of the new Euro currency. There are 100 cents in one Euro.

The Council of Europe

The Council of Europe is not part of the E.U. It is a European organization that exists to protect human rights in Europe. It has 41 members, many more than the E.U. The citizens of any of its member states can appeal to the European Court, run by the Council of Europe, if they feel they are not being treated fairly by the legal system in their own country.

The E.U. flag has 12 stars representing the 12 states which were members when the E.U. was named in 1993.

Euro-skeptics

Although belonging to European organizations brings benefits, it may also have disadvantages. Some people in Europe are worried that the increasing power of European organizations could threaten the unique culture of individual countries. In several countries, political activists, sometimes called Euro-skeptics, campaign to stop their governments from signing up to European laws and joining the single currency.

These are farmers from all over Europe protesting in Strasbourg against some of the European Union's agricultural policies.

Zulu men wearing traditional headdresses for a celebration in Durban, South Africa

AFRICA

AFRICA

Africa is a huge continent, the second biggest in the world. It has over 50 countries, hundreds of peoples and many different religions and ways of life. Yet many Africans also have a sense of belonging together as one big group, especially in the part of the continent south of the Sahara Desert.

This map shows where Africa is.

Freedom

In the 15th century, Europeans began to transport people from West Africa to Europe and North and South America to work as slaves. Slavery was abolished in the 19th century, but European countries then began to take over Africa for themselves. Most of the continent was divided into colonies ruled by Portugal, Belgium, Italy, France, Britain and Germany. Native Africans resisted foreign rule, and most African countries became independent in the 1960s and 1970s.

Africa's peoples

Africa has hundreds of ethnic groups each with its own culture, religion, language and traditions. One country can contain many different peoples, while a single ethnic group can spread across several countries.

A South African dancer wearing traditional dress

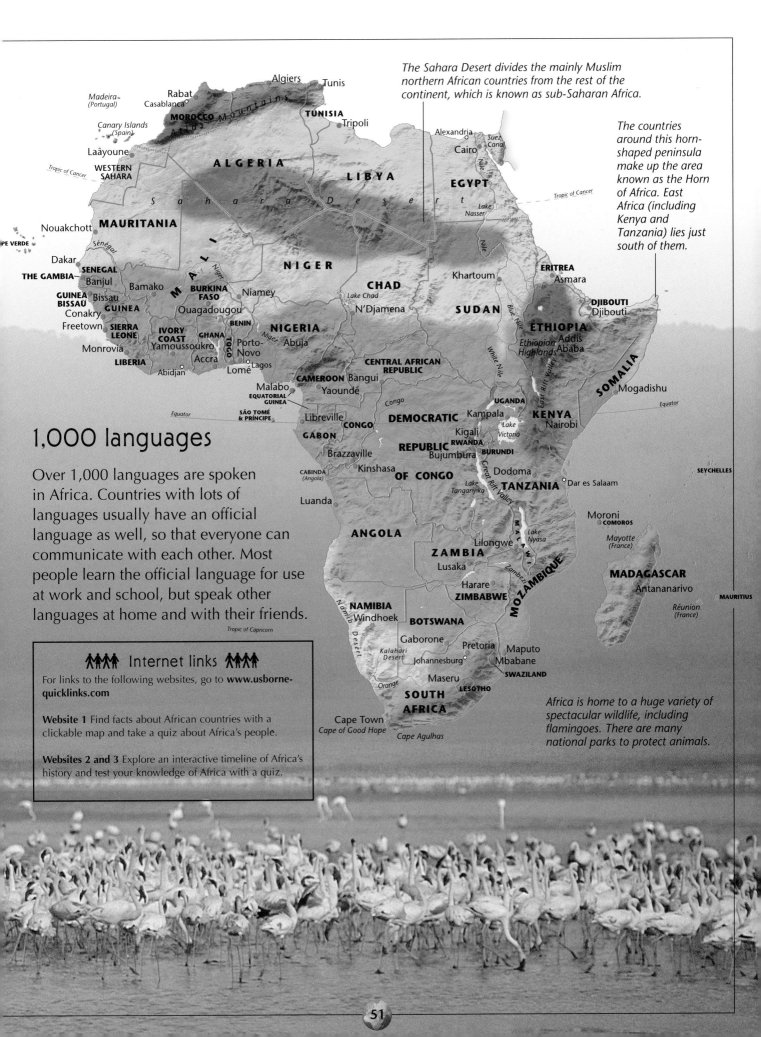

The Sahara Desert divides the mainly Muslim northern African countries from the rest of the continent, which is known as sub-Saharan Africa.

The countries around this horn-shaped peninsula make up the area known as the Horn of Africa. East Africa (including Kenya and Tanzania) lies just south of them.

Madeira
(Portugal)

Canary Islands
(Spain)

Tropic of Cancer

Laâyoune

WESTERN
SAHARA

Rabat
Casablanca
MOROCCO
Algiers
Tunis
TUNISIA
Tripoli

Atlas Mountains

ALGERIA

LIBYA

EGYPT

Alexandria
Cairo
Suez Canal

Tropic of Cancer

Lake Nasser

Nile

MAURITANIA
Nouakchott

Sahara Desert

NIGER

CHAD

SUDAN
Khartoum

ERITREA
Asmara

DJIBOUTI
Djibouti

Sénégal

Dakar
SENEGAL
THE GAMBIA
Banjul
Bamako
GUINEA
BISSAU
Bissau
GUINEA
Conakry
SIERRA
LEONE
Freetown
Monrovia
LIBERIA

MALI
BURKINA
FASO
Ouagadougou
Niamey

BENIN
NIGERIA
Abuja
N'Djamena
Lake Chad

Niger

IVORY
COAST
GHANA
Yamoussoukro
Abidjan
TOGO
Accra
Porto-Novo
Lomé
Lagos

CAMEROON
Bangui
Yaoundé
Malabo
EQUATORIAL
GUINEA

CENTRAL AFRICAN
REPUBLIC

Blue Nile

White Nile

ETHIOPIA
Ethiopian
Highlands
Addis
Ababa

SOMALIA
Mogadishu

Equator

SÃO TOMÉ
& PRÍNCIPE
Libreville
CONGO
GABON
Brazzaville

Congo

DEMOCRATIC

REPUBLIC

OF CONGO

Kampala
UGANDA
Kigali
RWANDA
Bujumbura
BURUNDI

Lake
Victoria

KENYA
Nairobi

East Rift Valley

Equator

CABINDA
(Angola)
Kinshasa
Luanda

Dodoma
TANZANIA

Lake
Tanganyika

Great Rift Valley

Dar es Salaam

SEYCHELLES

1,000 languages

Over 1,000 languages are spoken in Africa. Countries with lots of languages usually have an official language as well, so that everyone can communicate with each other. Most people learn the official language for use at work and school, but speak other languages at home and with their friends.

ANGOLA

ZAMBIA
Lusaka

Lilongwe
Lake
Nyasa

MALAWI

Zambezi

MOZAMBIQUE

Moroni
COMOROS

Mayotte
(France)

MADAGASCAR
Antananarivo

MAURITIUS

Réunion
(France)

Tropic of Capricorn

Harare
ZIMBABWE

Namib Desert

NAMIBIA
Windhoek

BOTSWANA
Gaborone

Kalahari
Desert
Johannesburg

Pretoria
Maputo
Mbabane
SWAZILAND

👫👫 Internet links 👫👫

For links to the following websites, go to www.usborne-quicklinks.com

Website 1 Find facts about African countries with a clickable map and take a quiz about Africa's people.

Websites 2 and 3 Explore an interactive timeline of Africa's history and test your knowledge of Africa with a quiz.

Maseru
LESOTHO

SOUTH
AFRICA

Orange

Cape Town
Cape of Good Hope
Cape Agulhas

Africa is home to a huge variety of spectacular wildlife, including flamingoes. There are many national parks to protect animals.

PEOPLES AND POWER

Africa was once made up of ethnic kingdoms, each with its own language and culture. But when European powers split Africa into countries, the new borders ran across the kingdoms of peoples such as the Tuareg and the Masai, dividing up their homelands.

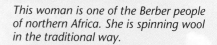

This woman is one of the Berber people of northern Africa. She is spinning wool in the traditional way.

Ethnic emphasis

Africans often feel that their ethnic group is just as important as their nationality. Instead of just being Ghanaian or Kenyan, for example, Africans may introduce themselves as Yoruba, Bantu, Mundani, San, Berber, or one of hundreds of other groups.

Wars and civil wars

After countries such as Chad, Nigeria and Angola gained independence from Europe, different ethnic groups began to fight for power. Many of the wars still going on in Africa are based on ethnic disagreements. Often, as in the conflict between Hutu and Tutsi peoples in Rwanda and Burundi in the 1990s,

people on the losing side end up fleeing across borders to nearby countries. People who have been forced to find a new place to live are often called refugees (because they are seeking refuge, or safety).

This is a refugee camp in Rwanda. It provided a temporary shelter for thousands of people who were forced to leave home by the war there in 1994.

Local leaders

Although African countries are ruled by their governments, many villages and ethnic groups also have their own local leaders, or chiefs. A chief has the power to settle disputes, and presides over ceremonies and official celebrations. The role of chief is usually passed from father to son.

This is Togbui Adeladza II, the leader of the Anlo-Ewe people of Ghana, dressed in ceremonial clothing.

Internet links

For links to the following websites, go to **www.usborne-quicklinks.com**

Website 1 Find lots of information about life in Africa today.

Website 2 Photos and stories about water - an important resource in African countries.

Website 3 Meet Asamoah, a cocoa producer in Ghana.

Website 4 Visit four different schools in Africa.

The Nanas Benz of Togo

Women rarely gain political power in African governments. But some African peoples have matriarchal societies. This means that power is passed from mother to daughter. In parts of Togo, for example, rich female cloth traders called "Nanas Benz" are the most powerful people in their communities. They pass on their businesses and their wealth to their daughters. If they only have sons, they pass everything to their nieces instead.

DESERT LANDS

The Sahara, the world's biggest desert, divides northern Africa from the rest of the continent. The Mediterranean countries (Morocco, Algeria, Tunisia, Libya and Egypt) are Muslim nations. They tend to have more in common with the Middle East than with the rest of Africa.

These pendants represent the Hand of Fatima, the daughter of Mohammed who is the main prophet of Islam.

Life in the desert

The Sahara takes up over 70% of the land in northern Africa, though only a few people live there. These include the Tuareg, a nomadic people who looked after trade routes in the desert in ancient times. Because of severe droughts in the last few decades, many desert people have had to abandon their old lifestyles and move to the cities.

Fatima's hand

In Northern Africa, the Muslim religion is very important. Most people pray several times each day. They also protect themselves from bad luck with images of a patterned hand, called the Hand of Fatima. It is said to ward off the "evil eye", which means a curse caused by a jealous glance.

Traditionally, Tuareg men wear veils like these, which show only the eyes, in the presence of women and strangers.

Walled cities

In some modern northern African cities, such as Marrakesh in Morocco and Tunis in Tunisia, there are still old medieval towns, or *medinas*. Surrounded by tall, thick walls, these old towns are crammed with tiny winding streets, along which markets, or *souks*, are held. Different kinds of goods are sold or made in different areas of the town. For example, noisy or smelly trades such as leather-making take place near the edge of the town, while crafts such as bookbinding are close to the main mosque.

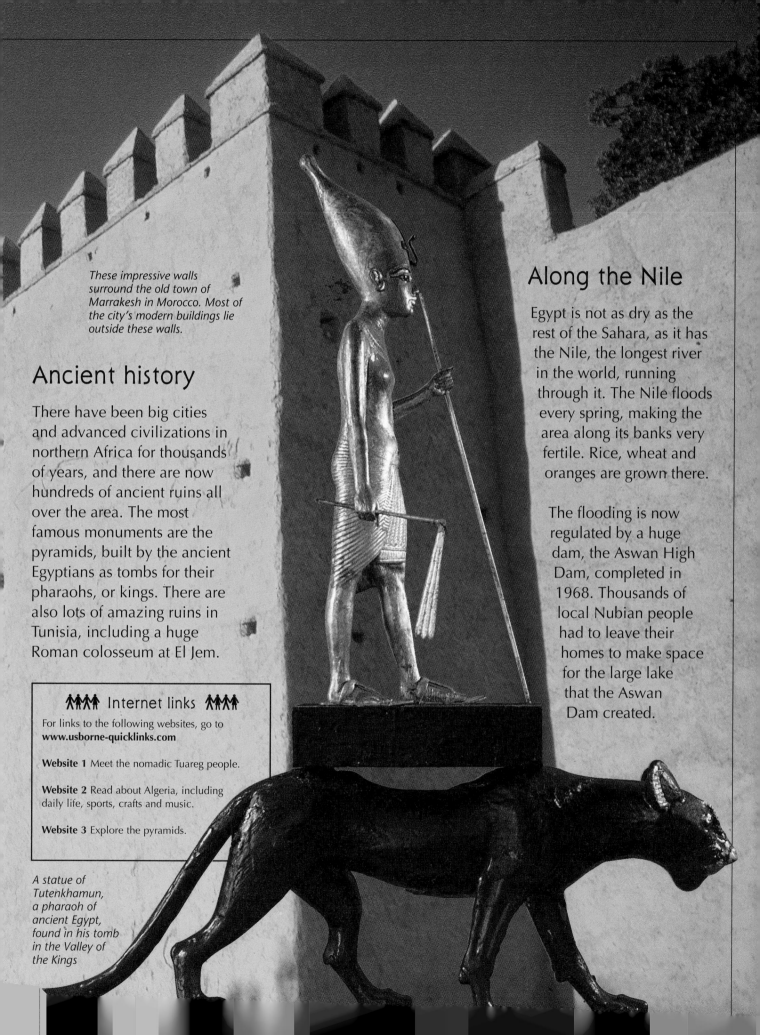

These impressive walls surround the old town of Marrakesh in Morocco. Most of the city's modern buildings lie outside these walls.

Ancient history

There have been big cities and advanced civilizations in northern Africa for thousands of years, and there are now hundreds of ancient ruins all over the area. The most famous monuments are the pyramids, built by the ancient Egyptians as tombs for their pharaohs, or kings. There are also lots of amazing ruins in Tunisia, including a huge Roman colosseum at El Jem.

👪👪 Internet links 👪👪

For links to the following websites, go to
www.usborne-quicklinks.com

Website 1 Meet the nomadic Tuareg people.

Website 2 Read about Algeria, including daily life, sports, crafts and music.

Website 3 Explore the pyramids.

A statue of Tutenkhamun, a pharaoh of ancient Egypt, found in his tomb in the Valley of the Kings

Along the Nile

Egypt is not as dry as the rest of the Sahara, as it has the Nile, the longest river in the world, running through it. The Nile floods every spring, making the area along its banks very fertile. Rice, wheat and oranges are grown there.

The flooding is now regulated by a huge dam, the Aswan High Dam, completed in 1968. Thousands of local Nubian people had to leave their homes to make space for the large lake that the Aswan Dam created.

WEST AND CENTRAL AFRICA

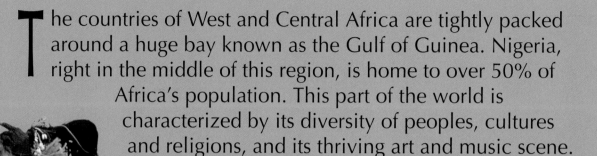

The countries of West and Central Africa are tightly packed around a huge bay known as the Gulf of Guinea. Nigeria, right in the middle of this region, is home to over 50% of Africa's population. This part of the world is characterized by its diversity of peoples, cultures and religions, and its thriving art and music scene.

The Sahel

The Sahel is a strip of dry land south of the Sahara Desert. Countries there, such as Chad, Niger and Mali, are cut off from the coast and have little fertile land. Bad droughts happen every few years. Nomadic herders, such as the Tuareg, live in the north of the Sahel. In the south, the land is greener and people live by farming and fishing.

Left: Dogon people dance on stilts at a traditional celebration in the village of Sangha, Mali.

Along the coast

The small countries along the western African coast, such as Ghana, Liberia and Senegal, are among Africa's wealthier nations. As well as farming and fishing, many of them mine valuable deposits of iron ore, diamonds and gold. Having been ruled by Europe, these countries gained their independence in the mid-20th century. But some, such as Sierra Leone, have been damaged by wars between groups battling for power.

Nigeria

Nigeria is the most populated country in Africa. It is a land of huge diversity, from the high-rise coastal city of Lagos to tropical forests in the east, and dusty plains and mud-walled villages in the central regions. Nigeria also has many different peoples, belonging to over 300 ethnic groups. The three biggest groups are the mainly-Muslim Hausa and Fulani peoples of the north, the Christian Igbo of the south, and the southwestern Yoruba people, most of whom follow traditional local religions.

This statue is part of a Yoruba shrine in Oshogbo, southwestern Nigeria, dedicated to a river goddess called Oshun.

👥👥 Internet links 👥👥

For links to websites where you can meet the peoples of the Sahel, listen to the songs of the Dogon people, and learn some Nigerian words with an online matching game, go to **www.usborne-quicklinks.com**

A street in Lagos, Nigeria's biggest city with a population of over 10 million people, bustles with cars, buses, pedestrians and busy markets.

These Buduma people are fishing from a papyrus reed boat. The Buduma live on a series of islands in Lake Chad, which is between Chad, Niger, Nigeria and Cameroon.

Diverse religions

Across Africa, many ancient, local belief systems are still strong. They often involve animism, a belief in spirits belonging to plants or animals. The spirit world is believed to exist alongside the physical world and to be able to affect it in various ways.

LANDSCAPES OF THE EAST

Africa's most famous landscapes are found along its eastern side, where deserts in the north give way to grasslands, lakes and wildlife reserves in the Great Rift Valley. This region has been influenced by many peoples, including Indians, Arabs, and local ethnic groups such as the Masai.

Eastern Africa has huge expanses of open grasslands which are home to many large animals, such as lions.

The Horn of Africa

The Horn of Africa is a hook-shaped piece of land sticking out into the sea just south of Arabia. The countries there, such as Ethiopia, Djibouti and Somalia, are hot and dry, and most people live by herding cattle from place to place.

Recently Ethiopia and Somalia have suffered from famines, triggered by droughts which have killed crops and farm animals. Money has often been spent on wars instead of food, and areas have become so dangerous that aid workers are unable to reach them.

Ecotourism

In Kenya and Tanzania, the Great Rift Valley's grassy plains teem with leopards, lions, antelopes and other wildlife. These countries have set aside huge national parks and reserves, which not only protect the animals, but also make money from tourism. In the past, people paid to hunt these animals, but now tourists go on safaris to spot and photograph them.

The round, thatched huts in this farming village near Belet Weyne, Somalia, are typical traditional East African homes. There is also a pen for the cattle.

Losing a lake

The peoples who live around Lake Victoria, which straddles Uganda, Tanzania and Kenya, have fished in the lake and used it as a way to get around for centuries. But recently Lake Victoria has been polluted by fertilizers running into it from coffee and tea fields, and the amount of fish in it has fallen.

Great Rift Valley

The Great Rift Valley is made up of a huge series of valleys and lakes which stretch all the way down East Africa. The lakes and fertile hillsides make this a good area for fishing and farming. Archaeologists searching there have found skulls and tools which suggest that East Africa was the home of the first ever human beings.

The Masai

East Africa is home to many local ethnic groups. The Masai, who live in Tanzania and Kenya, are proud of their nomadic cattle-herding lifestyle. They rarely slaughter their cattle for food. Instead, they get protein by drinking milk and blood drawn from the cattle.

Today, Masai people also visit towns to sell their cattle and buy goods. Some also make money by selling their famous beadwork and posing in traditional dress for tourists.

 Internet links

For links to the following websites, go to
www.usborne-quicklinks.com

Website 1 Meet a young Masai boy called Dita and read about his daily life.

Website 2 Find photos about life in Kenya and try a Swahili picture puzzle.

Website 3 Play a photo safari game.

A young Masai woman dressed up in a traditional beadwork headdress, necklaces and earrings

SOUTHERN AFRICA

Southern Africa is a region of rich farmland, dusty deserts, beautiful coasts and steamy swamps. It is dominated by South Africa, Africa's richest country. South Africa's mines, farms and factories provide work for many people from other southern African countries. Yet South Africa itself is in the midst of huge changes.

The mining of precious stones such as diamonds creates jobs for many people in South Africa.

Divisions and inequality

In 1994, South Africa held its first free election after more than 40 years of a regime known as apartheid. Under apartheid (which means "apartness"), only white people could vote. They ruled the country, and the main ethnic groups were forced to live separately from each other.

At the election, a party called the African National Congress was voted into power and things began to change. People of all ethnic groups can now live and work together. But there are big inequalities, and many South Africans still struggle with poverty, violence and a high crime rate.

Nelson Mandela was a leading member of South Africa's anti-apartheid movement. He was the country's president from 1994 to 1999.

Diamonds and gold

A lot of southern Africa's wealth comes from its rich deposits of valuable minerals. The world's biggest goldfield is in Witwatersrand, near Johannesburg in South Africa, and thousands of people across southern Africa work in mines extracting precious stones and metals.

Internet links

For links to websites where you can find out about the lives of the Zulu, Xhosa and San peoples, and visit an online exhibit about the life of Nelson Mandela, go to **www.usborne-quicklinks.com**

!Kung San

The Kalahari is a stony desert which occupies parts of Botswana, South Africa and Namibia. It has been home to the !Kung San people for several thousand years. Many have moved to the cities, but a few still live as hunter-gatherers. The men hunt wild animals, while the women and children collect nuts, fruit and honey.

The !Kung San, along with many other southern African peoples, speak a language belonging to a group called Khoisan languages. As well as vowels and consonants, the languages include clicking noises made with the tongue. The ! sign stands for just one of many different types of click.

Hunter-gatherers, like these !Kung San picking berries in the Kalahari, have one of the world's oldest lifestyles.

Island life

Two young boys from Madagascar carrying a fishing net. Fishing is an important part of island life.

To the east of southern Africa lie the islands of Madagascar, Mauritius, Comoros and the Seychelles. The first people to live there came from Southeast Asia, over 4,000km (2,500 miles) away across the Indian Ocean. Today, the people are a mix of African, south Asian and Arabic ethnic groups. They make a living from fishing and tourism, and from growing spices.

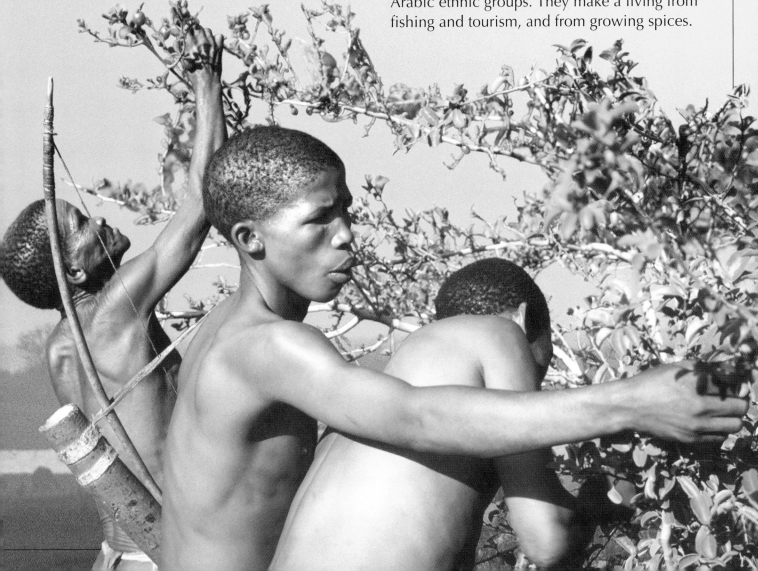

AFRICAN ART

Africa is famous for its arts and crafts of all kinds: sculpture and mask-making, painting, beadwork, pottery and carving. Traditionally, African artworks were used in religious ceremonies or worn on special occasions. Today, they are also sold to tourists, exported, or shown in art galleries.

Prehistoric pictures

8,000-year-old rock paintings and engravings found in the Sahara Desert are the earliest examples of African art. The hunting scenes in these pictures suggest that the Sahara was once much greener than it is today, with more people and wildlife living in it.

A prehistoric rock painting found in Tassili, Algeria, showing people with a herd of cattle

Masks and statues

Masks and statues are much more common in African art than pictures of landscapes or objects. This is because African art is often designed for use in ceremonies. Masks and statues can show gods, spirits, or images of perfect beauty, and can also be used for good luck. Some Ashanti women in Ghana, for example, carry a figure of a baby as a charm to help them have healthy children.

This mask is from Zimbabwe. It is part of a ceremonial dancing costume.

62

Symbolic coffins

In Accra, Ghana's capital city, an unusual art form has developed. Those who can afford it can be buried in special coffins built to represent their lifestyles. For example, a businessman might have a car-shaped coffin or a fisherman could have a fish or boat-shaped coffin.

This chicken-shaped coffin was probably built for a farmer.

👫👫 Internet links 👫👫

For links to the following websites, go to **www.usborne-quicklinks.com**

Website 1 Learn about life in Africa by looking at artwork.

Website 2 Find out about Adinkra, an African fabric.

Websites 3 and 4 Design your own African mask and learn how to draw like an Egyptian.

Body art

Earrings and nose rings, face painting and elaborate hairstyles are vital elements of many traditional ceremonies. Some peoples also use tattooing and scarification (marking the skin with scars) to create a kind of body art.

Women of the Nuer people of southern Sudan have their faces patterned with scars to mark their passage into adulthood.

Ancient Egyptian artworks, like this 3,300-year-old carving in Saqqara, attract many tourists to Africa every year.

63

Children carry balloons and flowers at the opening ceremony of a school in Hanoi, Vietnam

ASIA

ASIA

Asia is the world's biggest continent. It covers almost a third of the Earth's land surface, and over 60% of the world's people live there. Asian peoples are very diverse, with hundreds of different cultures, lifestyles, religions and political systems.

This map shows where Asia is.

More than three-quarters of Russia is in Asia, but the rest is part of Europe. The Ural Mountains divide the two parts.

Turkey is mostly in Asia, but part of it is in Europe.

Asia's richest oil deposits are found in the Middle East, the most westerly part of Asia.

Asia

Pacific Ocean

Indian Ocean

Australasia

Arctic Circle

Wrangel Island

New Siberia Islands

Severnaya Zemlya

Novaya Zemlya

Siberia

Kamchatka

St. Petersburg

Moscow

Ob

Yenisey

Lena

Yakutsk

RUSSIA

Sakhalin

Arctic Circle

Volgograd

Ural Mountains

Astana

Lake Baikal

Amur

Ankara
Izmir
Black Sea
TURKEY
GEORGIA
Nicosia
CYPRUS
LEBANON
Beirut
ISRAEL
SYRIA
Jerusalem
JORDAN
Amman
Damascus
IRAQ
Baghdad
Tbilisi
Yerevan
ARMENIA
Baku
AZERBAIJAN
Caspian Sea
Volga
Steppes
KAZAKSTAN
Aral Sea
UZBEKISTAN
Tashkent
TURKMENISTAN
Tehran
Ashgabat
Bishkek
KYRGYZSTAN
Dushanbe
TAJIKISTAN
Tien Shan
Altai Mts.
Ulan Bator
MONGOLIA
Gobi Desert
Shenyang
Vladivostok
N. KOREA
Pyongyang
Seoul
S. KOREA
JAPAN
Tokyo
Osaka
Beijing (Peking)
Tianjin
Huang He

Tropic of Cancer
IRAN
KUWAIT
Kuwait
SAUDI ARABIA
Riyadh
BAHRAIN
QATAR
Doha
UNITED ARAB EMIRATES
Abu Dhabi
AFGHANISTAN
Kabul
Islamabad
PAKISTAN
Indus
Karachi
Himalaya Mountains
NEPAL
Delhi
New Delhi
Kathmandu
BHUTAN
Thimphu
Plateau of Tibet
CHINA
Wuhan
Chongqing
Yangtze
Shanghai
Tropic of Cancer
Taipei
TAIWAN
Guangzhou (Canton)
Hong Kong

Muscat
OMAN
Sana
YEMEN
INDIA
Ganges
Dhaka
BANGLA-DESH
Kolkata (Calcutta)
MYANMAR (BURMA)
Hanoi
VIETNAM
LAOS
Manila
PHILIPPINES
Mumbai (Bombay)
Socotra (Yemen)
MALDIVES
Colombo
SRI LANKA
Andaman Islands (India)
Vientiane
Yangon (Rangoon)
THAILAND
Bangkok
CAMBODIA
Phnom Penh
Ho Chi Minh
Mekong
Nicobar Islands (India)
Kuala Lumpur
Medan
Sumatra
MALAYSIA
Putrajaya
SINGAPORE
Borneo
BRUNEI
Bandar Seri Begawan
Sulawesi (Celebes)
Equator
Equator
INDONESIA
Palembang
Jakarta
Java
Surabaya
EAST TIMOR

New states

Since 1991, Asia has gained more than ten new states, including Tajikistan, Kyrgyzstan and Kazakstan. These were once part of the U.S.S.R. (Union of Soviet Socialist Republics), a huge country governed from Moscow. In 1991 the U.S.S.R. dissolved into several independent states, including Russia, which is still the biggest country in the world.

Nomads from Mongolia set up temporary camps as they move around. They live in circular tents like this.

Big business

Asia is home to some of the world's biggest banking, manufacturing and trading nations. Wealthy cities such as Hong Kong, Tokyo, Singapore, Dubai, Bahrain and Kuala Lumpur tower with gleaming skyscrapers.

Many of the things you own, especially clothes, computers, toys, phones and CDs, have probably been made in Asia. Millions of factory workers in countries such as Korea, China, Taiwan and Japan make goods to be exported and sold all over the world.

Farming and fishing

Asia has thousands and thousands of miles of coastline, especially in the southeast, where there are over 15,000 islands. Because of this, fishing has become a vital source of food and work for millions of Asians.

The continent has vast areas of fertile farmland, with millions of tiny farms where poor families grow food for their own use. But Asia also has large farms that export crops such as rice, rubber, tea and coffee around the world.

This structure is a traditional Chinese fishing net. These types of nets have been used for hundreds of years. The net is dipped into the water using a long pole.

👫👫 Internet links 👫👫

For links to the following websites, go to **www.usborne-quicklinks.com**

Website 1 Explore an interactive map of Asia, with pictures, sound clips and facts.

Website 2 Take a lesson in Japanese and find out more about the food, history and culture of Japan.

Website 3 Find out about the importance of rice in Asia then try to build a rice paddy online.

Website 4 Try the ancient Japanese art of paper folding - origami.

Website 5 Explore some Asian countries, with fact files and photos.

A RANGE OF RELIGIONS

All the world's major religions started in Asia. The continent still has a wide range of religions and many of them, such as Christianity, Islam and Judaism, have also spread around the world. For billions of Asians, religious rituals are an essential everyday activity.

Holy places

Important holy sites are found all over Asia. They include places where prophets were born or died, places where religions began, and cities, mountains and rivers that are believed to be sacred. Millions of people from all over the world make religious journeys, or pilgrimages, to these sites every year.

Holy water

The Ganges River in northern India is sacred to Hindus, who make up 90% of India's population. Pilgrims visit the Ganges to purify themselves by bathing in its waters, and religious ceremonies are often held on its banks.

These women are bathing at dawn in the Ganges River at Varanasi, India. Special steps have been built there so pilgrims can get in and out of the water safely.

A trip to Mecca

All Muslims are expected to make a pilgrimage (or *Hajj*) to the holy city of Mecca, in Saudi Arabia, at least once in their lives. It is the birthplace of Mohammed, the prophet of Islam. When they arrive, the pilgrims walk around a shrine called the Ka'bah, which is said to have been built by the prophet Ibrahim.

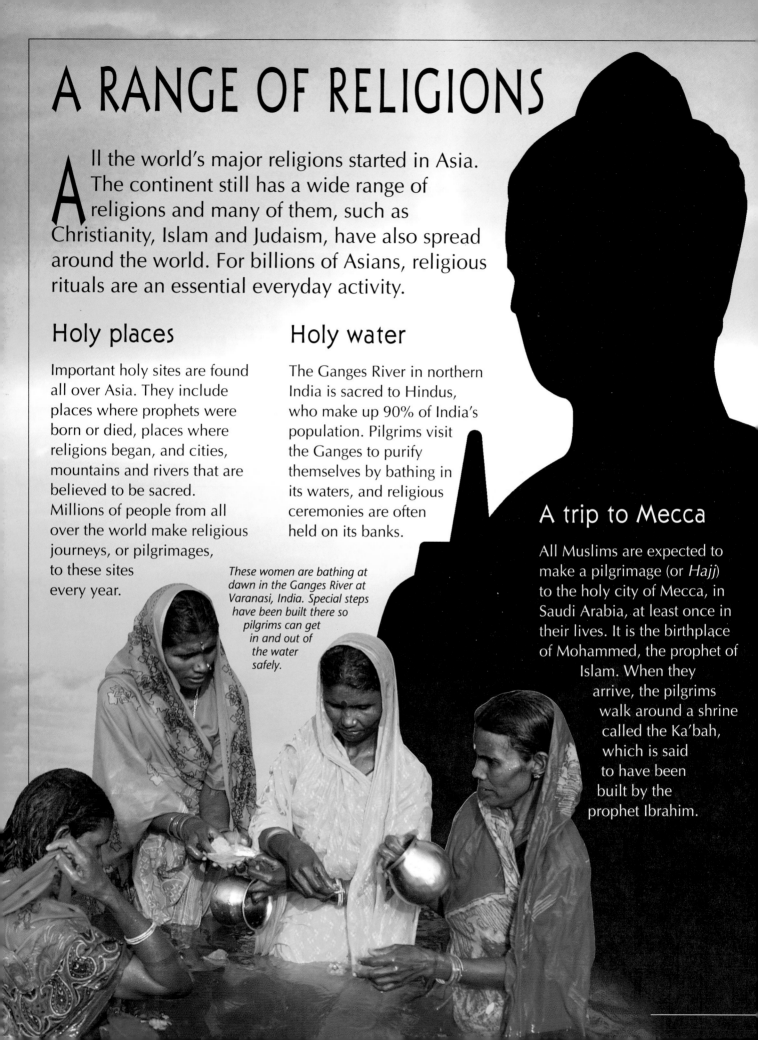

Jerusalem

Jerusalem is a holy city for Jews, Christians and Muslims. It contains the Western Wall, the remains of a Jewish temple, and the Dome of the Rock, a shrine marking the spot where the Islam prophet Mohammed is said to have risen into heaven. It is also where Christians believe Jesus Christ, the founder of Christianity, was crucified.

👫👫 Internet links 👫👫

For links to the following websites, go to
www.usborne-quicklinks.com

Website 1 Make your own pilgrimage to Mecca.

Websites 2 and 3 Learn more about Jerusalem's holy sites and watch video clips of Muslim prayers.

The silhouette in the background is part of the huge Borobudur Buddhist temple in Java, Indonesia.

Jewish pilgrims visit the Western Wall to mourn the destruction of their temple, and to insert prayers into cracks in the wall. In the background is the Dome of the Rock, part of a Muslim shrine.

Beautiful buildings

There are beautiful religious buildings all over Asia: Muslim mosques, Sikh gurdwaras, Christian churches, Hindu temples, and Buddhist pagodas. Many of these holy buildings have been created by the very best craftspeople, using expensive and gorgeous materials. Their impressive shapes often dominate cities' skylines.

Spiritual sounds

In Asia, many people take part in regular religious chanting, praying or singing. For example, Muslims are called to prayer five times a day, many Buddhists chant verses every day, and dancing and singing are an important part of Hindu ceremonies.

This man is calling Muslims to prayer. An official who does this is called a muezzin.

RUSSIA

Russia is the world's biggest country. It covers 11% of the Earth's land surface, stretches across eight time zones and straddles two continents: Europe and Asia. It takes over a week to travel by train from St. Petersburg in the west to Vladivostok in the east.

These are matryoshka *dolls, which open up into halves so that several dolls can fit one inside the other. The word* matryoshka *means mother in Russian.*

City culture

Russia's cities are famous across the world for their art and culture. Moscow and St. Petersburg (which are both in European Russia) have dozens of beautiful museums and palaces. Russia is also home to world-famous orchestras and ballet companies such as Moscow's Bolshoi Ballet.

This is St. Basil's Cathedral, Moscow. The beautiful onion-shaped domes are characteristic of Russian church architecture.

Big changes

The independent country of Russia, officially known as the Russian Federation, has only existed since 1991. Before that, it belonged to the U.S.S.R. This was an even bigger country, created in 1917 when a Communist revolution overthrew the Russian czar, or king. For most of the 20th century, Communists ran the U.S.S.R.

Communism

Communism is a way of running a country. Under Communism, the state owns everything, including railways, roads, factories and houses, and it distributes things like food, money and medicine among the people. It is the opposite of Capitalism, in which people can own their own houses and run their own businesses. The government which ruled the U.S.S.R. from 1917 to 1991 was the world's best-known Communist system.

This girl is playing outside the tent where her family lives, in Chukchi, in the far northeast of Russia.

Size matters

Russia is over 10,000km (6,100 miles) across. When it's bedtime in the west, people in the east are just waking up. People in different parts of the country have very different lifestyles, depending on the climate and landscape where they live, and the influence of nearby countries. In the north, Russia extends beyond the Arctic Circle, but few people live there because it's too cold. There is a central government in Moscow, but many of Russia's regions have their own laws, parliaments and languages.

In some parts of Russia it can be extremely cold. These children live in the Kamchatka region where the average temperature is -40°C (-40°F).

New freedoms

Under Communism there were strict rules. Books and newspapers were tightly regulated, religion was suppressed and it was hard to leave the country. In 1991, the Communists were defeated and the U.S.S.R. broke up into 15 new countries. Many of the old rules were relaxed. However, the new freedoms also mean that crime has increased and many people are poorer than they were under Communism, because the state no longer looks after everyone.

Varied literature

Russian literature is well-known around the world. Russia's most famous writers include Dostoevsky, Tolstoy and Pushkin; they wrote realist novels. However Russia also has a rich tradition of magical folk tales and fairy tales, which have been passed down orally for centuries.

👪 Internet links 👪

For links to the following websites, go to **www.usborne-quicklinks.com**

Website 1 A fun guide to Russia.

Website 2 Go sightseeing in Moscow, the capital of Russia.

Website 3 Explore Russia's past with an interactive timeline.

THE MIDDLE EAST

The Middle East is famous for its beautiful old buildings and wealthy modern cities, and the hospitality of its peoples. It was where Sumer, the home of the first civilization, was; and it is the nucleus of the world's oil industry. It is sometimes seen as a trouble spot, because of the many wars and revolutions that have taken place there.

These are Marsh Arabs, a people from Iraq who live in houses built on floating platforms of reeds. They are loading mats made from reeds onto a truck.

This woman in Oman is wearing a mask to cover her face. Some Islamic women cover their faces in public to protect their modesty.

What is the Middle East?

The Middle East is usually said to include the area between the Red Sea and the Persian Gulf, as well as Israel, Jordan, Syria, Lebanon, Iran and Iraq. It was named the Middle East by Europeans, because it is east of Europe, but not as far away as other Asian countries such as China, Japan and Korea (often referred to as the Far East).

Different peoples

The peoples of the Middle East belong to four main groups: Arabs, Persians, Turks and Jews. The area's Arabic countries (Bahrain, Saudi Arabia, Yemen, Oman, Qatar, Kuwait and United Arab Emirates) lie in and around the peninsula of Arabia. Their people are Muslims and speak Arabic languages. But Iran, once known as Persia, is not Arabic, and nor is Turkey, although they too are mainly Muslim. Israel is a Jewish state which was created in 1948. Many Arabs claim that Israel's land belongs to an Arabic people, the Palestinians.

Desert life

Stretching across the Middle East are vast deserts which contain important oil reserves. Few people live in these areas. However, some Bedouin herders still travel across the desert from one oasis to the next with their animals. They use either camels or four-wheel-drive vehicles to carry their tents and possessions.

Bedouin people are nomads who traditionally live in the desert. These Bedouins are leading a train of camels.

Ancient & modern

When oil was discovered in the Middle East, it made many nations rich. They were able to rebuild their cities with new apartments and skyscrapers, and to provide for new banks and businesses. But most cities still have old areas with narrow streets and traditional markets, called souks.

These huge towers in Kuwait are for water storage. Kuwait is a desert nation with no rivers or lakes, so sea water has to be processed to make it safe to drink, then stored.

Coffee & small talk

Coffee probably first came from Yemen, in southern Arabia, and it is still an important part of life in the Middle East. When Middle Eastern people have visitors, they usually offer them coffee, along with dates or pieces of cake called baklava. Then, even if there is something important to discuss, it is polite to make small talk over coffee before getting down to business.

This is the traditional Middle Eastern way of pouring coffee, holding the pot up high to create a long, fine flow.

Internet links

For links to the following websites, go to **www.usborne-quicklinks.com**

Website 1 Meet Sa`ud, a boy from Kuwait.

Website 2 Find out about different Middle Eastern countries.

Website 3 The conflict between the Israelis and Palestinians.

CHINA

Nearly a quarter of the people on Earth are Chinese, and China is one of the world's oldest nations. It has existed for nearly 2,000 years, and had one of the earliest civilizations. The ancient Chinese invented paper, silk, gunpowder and seismology, the science of predicting earthquakes.

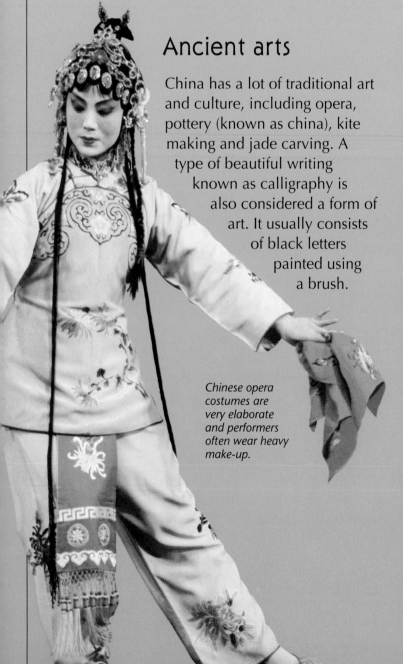

In Chinese cities people often use pedal power to get around. These children are riding in a wooden trailer on the back of a tricycle.

Ancient arts

China has a lot of traditional art and culture, including opera, pottery (known as china), kite making and jade carving. A type of beautiful writing known as calligraphy is also considered a form of art. It usually consists of black letters painted using a brush.

Chinese opera costumes are very elaborate and performers often wear heavy make-up.

Population explosion

In 1982, China became the first country to have over a billion (one thousand million) people. It now has over 1.3 billion. It is hard for China to provide enough food, schools and doctors for all its people. Since the 1950s, the government has tried to slow down the population increase. Couples are encouraged to get married later in life, and to have only one child.

Farming nation

Even though China has a lot of big cities, nearly three-quarters of its people live in the countryside and live by farming. Their main crops are rice, wheat and millet.

China is mountainous, and only about 10% of its land is fertile, so all the soil has to be used carefully. Terraces built into hillsides allow farmers to grow crops on steep slopes. Throughout China, farmland is irrigated, or watered, using systems of canals and streams.

Chinese beliefs

Many people in China follow Confucianism, a way of behaving based on the ideas of Confucius, who lived in China from 551-479BCE. He taught that people should be polite, considerate and obey their elders.

The ancient Chinese worshipped their ancestors and various gods. These old beliefs are remembered at certain times of the year. For example, many families keep a picture of the kitchen god next to their kitchen stove. Just before the New Year, they take down the picture and smear honey and wine on the god's lips to keep him happy. When the New Year arrives, a new picture is put up.

This is a holder for burning incense sticks. They give off a scent which is said to attract the attention of the gods.

New Year

The start of the Chinese year, which is usually in February, is marked with celebrations, including fireworks, parades and feasts. People decorate their homes with symbols of good fortune and unmarried people receive red envelopes containing money for good luck.

Internet links

For links to the following websites, go to **www.usborne-quicklinks.com**

Website 1 Explore an interactive guide to China, see famous landmarks and try a quiz.

Website 2 Get your own Chinese name and see how numbers are written in Chinese.

Spellings

Chinese writing uses symbols, or characters, to represent words. In other languages, Chinese words have to be written down as they sound. Recently these spellings have been changed to make them more consistent, so you might see different spellings in different books.

The Chinese characters on the right spell out the phrase "Peoples of the World".

世界各民族

The final day of Chinese New Year celebrations culminates in the Lantern Festival, where elaborate lanterns like this dragon lantern are carried along in a night-time procession.

Chinese writing, 25; Communism, 102

INDIA AND PAKISTAN

India and Pakistan straddle the area where, 4,500 years ago, a complex ancient society began in and around the Indus Valley. The two countries are now both modern states, but many of their people also follow ancient traditions and beliefs.

Pakistani truck, van and bus drivers are proud of their hand-decorated vehicles, like this truck covered in patterns and symbols.

Dividing into two countries

India and Pakistan used to be one country, which was ruled by Britain in the 19th century. Britain agreed to grant India its independence in 1947, but Hindus and Muslims wanted their own separate states. So the country was divided into two parts: Pakistan for the Muslims, and India for the more numerous Hindus. At first, Bangladesh was part of Pakistan, but it too became independent in 1971.

East and West

Britain's influence can be seen all over India and Pakistan. European-style buildings from the time of British rule stand among mosques and temples. Cricket, originally an English game, is an important sport in both India and Pakistan.

Indians and Pakistanis wear a mixture of European-style clothes and traditional dress, such as the *shalwar kameez* (baggy shirt and trousers) in Pakistan and the sari, a wrap-around gown, in India.

These women are from Rajasthan, in India. When walking long distances with awkward loads like these it is easiest to carry them on the head.

The building in the background is the Taj Mahal, near the city of Agra. It is an elaborate marble tomb built by a 17th-century Indian emperor, Shah Jahan, for his wife.

Film fanatics

India has the world's biggest film industry, based in Bombay and known as "Bollywood". Bollywood films are usually love stories or historical dramas, with lots of songs and dance routines. The top film stars and singers are incredibly rich and famous.

Getting around

In crowded cities such as Lahore and Calcutta, the streets are full of buses, trams, taxis, rickshaws and bikes jostling for space with pedestrians and market stalls. In India, cows wander the streets as well. Hindus regard cows as sacred animals and no one is allowed to harm them, so they slow down the traffic as everyone tries to keep out of their way.

Posters in Bombay advertising Bollywood films

👪 Internet links 👪

For links to the following websites, go to www.usborne-quicklinks.com

Website 1 Explore India with slide shows, stories and online activities.

Websites 2 and 3 Learn how to put on a sari and find a guide to Bollywood.

A rickshaw is a kind of open-air taxi. Rickshaws can be motorized or driven by pedal power. When a pedal rickshaw comes to a hill, the passengers get out and push it.

Caste

In Indian tradition, most people are born with a *Jati*, or caste, an inherited status. In ancient India, it determined the job you did, and you could only marry someone from the same group. *Jati* is still important to many people and people of the same *Jati* support each other. But some of the old laws have been abolished, so that Indians from all levels of society can hold positions of power.

Curry craze

Spicy food from Pakistan and India is popular across the globe. Its name "curry" comes from *kari*, from the Tamil language of southern India. Curry is usually vegetables or meat with a sauce, eaten with rice or bread. Hindus avoid eating meat, so Indian food is often vegetarian.

SOUTHEAST ASIA

Southeast Asia stretches out into the sea to the south of China and Japan. The countries there, including Thailand, Vietnam, Laos, Malaysia and Indonesia, are spread out over a long peninsula and a series of hilly, forested islands.

This is an Indonesian shadow puppet. It is moved using the rods attached to its arms and head.

This girl is performing a traditional dance, called the Legong, from Bali, in Indonesia.

Performing arts

Southeast Asia has a rich tradition of performing arts, often combining music, dance and drama. Performances are visually stunning, making use of masks and elaborate costumes.

In Indonesia, an unusual form of storytelling has developed which uses shadow puppets to tell the stories. The puppets are two-dimensional figures moved using rods. During a show, a light and a screen are placed behind them, so you can just see their silhouettes. A puppet's features reveal its character and status, so the audience is able to recognize key character types.

Temples and mosques

In Southeast Asia, many different religions exist side by side, usually peacefully. Some countries, such as Myanmar, are mainly Buddhist; others, such as Indonesia, are mainly Muslim; but other religions such as Christianity and Hinduism are also common. Temples, mosques and churches are found everywhere. There are also many ruined temples which have now been abandoned.

Internet links

For links to websites where you can watch animated puppet shows created by UK school children and meet Son, a boy who lives in Vietnam, go to **www.usborne-quicklinks.com**

Nations in pieces

Malaysia, Indonesia and the Philippines stretch across a vast archipelago (a network of islands) southeast of the Asian mainland. Even within the same country, different islands can be very unlike each other.

For example, Bali, one of Indonesia's most populated islands, is small and crowded, with farms, towns and a big tourist industry. Its main religion is a type of Hinduism, and it has thousands of temples. Irian Jaya, part of the much bigger island of New Guinea, is very remote, with thick forests. Most of its peoples live by farming, fishing and hunting. Some have converted to Christianity, while others worship the spirits of their

On the marshy eastern coast of Sumatra in Indonesia, men and boys spend part of the year fishing from huts on tall stilts built up to 10km (6 miles) out at sea.

Rice and spice

Although Southeast Asia has some big cities, most of its people are farmers and live in the countryside. Rice is their main crop and it forms a part of almost every meal.

Thailand and Indonesia are famous for their spicy food. Spices are not a major crop now, but hundreds of years ago they made this part of the world rich. Merchants came from India, Arabia, Europe and China to buy cloves, mace and nutmeg which were more valuable than gold.

Two girls in front of their thatched house in Western Samoa

AUSTRALASIA
AND OCEANIA

AUSTRALASIA AND OCEANIA

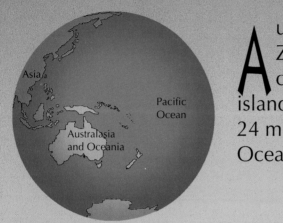

Asia

Pacific Ocean

Australasia and Oceania

Australasia is made up of Australia, New Zealand and Papua New Guinea. Oceania consists of the three main groups of Pacific islands: Melanesia, Micronesia and Polynesia. 24 million people live in Australasia, while Oceania is home to only about four million.

This map shows where Australasia and Oceania are.

Oceania is made up of thousands of islands.

The International Date Line is an imaginary line running through the Pacific Ocean. To the east of it, the date is a day earlier than it is to the west.

Northern Mariana Islands (U.S.A.)
Guam (U.S.A.)

MARSHALL ISLANDS

PALAU

Caroline Islands

FEDERATED STATES OF MICRONESIA

International Date Line

Line Islands

Equator

Equator

NAURU

Australia is the world's sixth largest country.

New Guinea

PAPUA NEW GUINEA

SOLOMON ISLANDS

KIRIBATI

Marquesas Islands

Cape York

Port Moresby

Honiara

TUVALU

Darwin

SAMOA

Society Islands

Tuamotu Archipelago

Great Barrier Reef

Port Vila

VANUATU

Suva

FIJI

Tahiti

FRENCH POLYNESIA

Great Sandy Desert

Alice Springs

Great Dividing Range

New Caledonia (France)

TONGA

Cook Islands (New Zealand)

Tropic of Capricorn

Tropic of Capricorn

AUSTRALIA

Lake Eyre

Pitcairn Islands (U.K.)

Great Victoria Desert

Brisbane

Perth

Nullarbor Plain

Darling

Cape Leeuwin

Adelaide

Murray

Sydney

Canberra

North Island

Auckland

New Zealand's main land area is made up of two islands.

Melbourne

NEW ZEALAND

Wellington

Tasmania

Hobart

Christchurch

South Island

Chatham Islands (New Zealand)

Early explorers

The first people to explore and inhabit Australasia and Oceania came originally from Southeast Asia. They include the Aborigines, who arrived in Australia between 40,000 and 60,000 years ago, the peoples who arrived on the Pacific islands about 7,000 years ago, and the Maoris, who arrived in New Zealand a little over 1,000 years ago.

Europeans arrive

In 1606, a Dutchman named Willem Jantszoon became the first European in Australia. In 1642, his countryman Abel Tasman was the first European to see New Zealand. An English explorer, James Cook, landed at Botany Bay, on the east coast of Australia in 1770. Eight years later the British established a penal colony there. During the 19th century, many parts of the Pacific were colonized by European countries. Today most Pacific nations have gained independence, but a few are still ruled by other countries.

This is the English explorer James Cook, who landed in Australia in 1770.

Many Pacific islanders still make the same type of wooden canoes that were used to sail to the area thousands of years ago.

ᴀᴀᴀ Internet links ᴀᴀᴀ

For links to the following websites, go to **www.usborne-quicklinks.com**

Website 1 Facts and maps of Oceania.

Website 2 View panoramic movies of Uluru and other Australian landscapes.

Uluru, formerly known as Ayers Rock, is a famous landmark in central Australia. It is a sacred site for Aborigines and Torres Strait islanders.

AUSTRALIA

Australia is bordered by the Pacific Ocean on one side and the Indian Ocean on the other. It is almost as big as Europe, yet has only 5% of the population Europe has. Most Australians live on the country's eastern and southeastern coasts.

Many people in the outback live a long way from a hospital, so a medical service known as the Flying Doctors rescues sick people by plane.

Australia's people

For many thousands of years the Aborigines and Torres Strait islanders were the only inhabitants of Australia. British colonists arrived in Australia in the 18th century, and in the 1850s gold was discovered. This brought a rush of people from Europe, China and the U.S.A., all hoping to make their fortunes by mining. In 1901 Australia ceased to be a set of colonies and became a nation. Today, it is mostly made up of people of British, Irish or Southeast Asian descent.

City life

Over 80% of Australia's population lives in cities and towns along the coast, as this is where jobs are to be found. Canberra is the capital, but Sydney is the biggest city. Over 4.5 million people, one-fifth of Australia's total population, live there. The other major Australian cities are Melbourne, Perth, Brisbane, Adelaide, Hobart and Darwin.

The outback

The vast desert area in the middle of Australia, known as the outback, is one of the hottest, driest places in the world. The soil is too dry for crops, but farmers keep sheep and cattle on enormous farms called stations, which can have 15,000 km² (5,800 square miles) or more of land. With farms and towns so far apart, people living in the outback can lead isolated lives. Children often live so far from the nearest school that lessons have to be held via the Internet, or transmitted by TV or radio.

Sydney's opera house sits on the edge of Sydney Harbour. Its roof mirrors the shape of the boats that sail past.

The coral reefs that make up the Great Barrier Reef support a huge variety of underwater life.

The first Australians

When the Aboriginal peoples came to Australia, they spread gradually across the country in large, nomadic groups, hunting animals and gathering plants. They believed that the land and its wildlife were sacred. When Europeans arrived, they seized much of the land for themselves, destroying many Aboriginal sacred places.

This Aboriginal man has painted his body and face as Aboriginal peoples have done for thousands of years. Body painting is a group activity and is usually done for special ceremonies.

Today, less than 2% of the Australian population is Aboriginal, and many no longer have a traditional lifestyle. They are just as likely to live in cities and have modern jobs. However, most Aboriginal peoples want to preserve their culture and, after years of campaigning, some traditional lands are now being returned to their original owners.

Sun, sea and sports

Australians enjoy their warm, sunny climate and spend a lot of time outdoors, playing sports, swimming, surfing and sailing. The climate and range of outdoor activities available also make Australia attractive as a tourist destination. Swimming and diving at Australia's Great Barrier Reef are especially popular, although scientists are concerned that too much tourism will damage the wildlife living around the reef.

⚇ Internet links

For links to the following websites, go to **www.usborne-quicklinks.com**

Website 1 Go sightseeing in Australia and learn some Australian slang.

Website 2 Take a virtual tour of Sydney Opera House.

Website 3 See lots of Aboriginal art.

Website 4 Listen to the sounds of a didgeridoo and learn how to play one.

NEW ZEALAND

New Zealand lies in the South Pacific, about 1,500km (1000 miles) southeast of Australia. The country is made up of two main islands, known as the North Island and the South Island, and several smaller ones. Much of New Zealand is wild and mountainous, and the country is sparsely populated, with fewer than four million people.

A young nation

New Zealand was one of the last places in the world to be inhabited. The first settlers, the Maoris, arrived around a thousand years ago, migrating from islands farther north. About 850 years later, Europeans began to arrive, and in 1840 New Zealand came under British rule. Today, it is an independent state. The majority of New Zealanders are still of British descent. The rest are mostly Maoris and South Sea islanders.

An experienced shearer can shear a sheep in just a few minutes. Wool is one of New Zealand's most important exports.

A land of farmers

Most New Zealanders make their living from farming. Over half the land is used for sheep farming and this is the country's biggest industry. Wool and lamb are major exports. Other exports include dairy products, wine, vegetables and fruit, such as oranges, lemons, grapefruits and kiwi fruit. New Zealand used to trade mainly with the U.K. but today much of its trade is with Australia and Asian countries.

This is a typical New Zealand sheep farm stretching over a vast area.

These tourists are photographing a geyser spouting hot water in Waiotapua Thermal Park.

Clean and green

New Zealand does not use nuclear power, and has little heavy industry and relatively small towns and cities. As a result, it is one of the world's least polluted countries. Its beautiful scenery attracts many tourists. In the North Island, active volcanoes and spouting geysers can be seen, and in the South Island, there are spectacular mountains with huge glaciers.

⋀⋀⋀ Internet links ⋀⋀⋀

For links to websites where you can watch a Maori welcome ceremony and find out more about Maori traditions, and take a photo tour of New Zealand, go to **www.usborne-quicklinks.com**

The Maoris

When they first arrived in New Zealand, the Maoris lived a traditional lifestyle. They hunted, fished and grew crops, and lived in small ethnic groups ruled by chiefs. Then in the early 19th century, British colonists arrived. Battles raged over who owned the land and many Maoris were killed. Most of those that were left were forced to move to the new towns and cities.

This Maori man has tattoos known as Ta Moko on his face. He is carrying a club called a wahaika, to take part in a traditional dance.

Modern Maoris

Today, Maoris make up about 10% of the population of New Zealand and their culture is being re-established. The Maori language is taught in schools and traditional arts such as tattooing (Ta Moko) have been revived. But many Maoris are still campaigning for the return of lands they lost. Their name for New Zealand is Aotearoa, which means "land of the long white clouds".

PAPUA NEW GUINEA

New Guinea, the world's second largest island after Greenland, lies in the Pacific Ocean, to the north of Australia. Its western half, called Irian Jaya, is part of Indonesia*. Its eastern half, together with around 600 small islands, makes up the country of Papua New Guinea.

🤾 Internet links 🤾

For links to websites where you can find facts about Papua New Guinea and send virtual postcards of tribal festivals, go to **www.usborne-quicklinks.com**

Peoples of Papua

Most Papua New Guineans are of Melanesian* origin, but there are also some Australians and a small Chinese population. The first inhabitants migrated from Southeast Asia over 40,000 years ago. They lived in small groups and found food by hunting and gathering.

The country is dominated by mountains and thick rainforests. This has meant that groups often became isolated. Today, there are still around a thousand different ethnic groups in Papua New Guinea.

Languages

Because there are so many separate groups, many different languages have developed in Papua New Guinea. There are more than 700 in total, a huge number of languages for a population of less than five million. The different groups communicate with each other in a language called Hiri Motu, or in pidgin English, which is a mixture of English and local languages. The official language is English, but in fact only 2% of the population can speak it.

This Waghi boy, from the eastern mountains of New Guinea, is wearing a traditional feather headdress for a festival at his high school in the town of Goroka.

*Indonesia, 79; Melanesia, 90

Village life

About a third of Papua New Guinea's people live in towns, where many have moved to find work. The rest still have a traditional lifestyle, similar to that of their ancestors. They live in villages, grow fruit and vegetables, catch fish and keep pigs and poultry. Some farmers sell their produce at local markets. Villagers eat a diet based on starchy crops such as sweet potatoes in the highland areas, and sago in the lowlands.

A father and son display their catch of fish for sale to passers-by.

These are men from a village called Asaro. They are wearing mud masks and their bodies are covered in mud too. Warriors of Asaro are said to have once dressed like this in order to win a battle, and villagers still sometimes dress like this today for tourists.

Art and life

The art of Papua New Guinea is a key part of local life, history and culture. Traditions vary from region to region and most forms of art have a practical or religious function.

In Malangan culture, groups make wooden masks to commemorate a death. The people of Kambot carve wooden story boards showing incidents from village life. Around the Gulf Province, shield-like objects called gope boards are hung outside houses. They are said to contain protective spirits which ward off sickness and evil. Many Papuan peoples also carve elaborate prows for canoes.

OCEANIA

S cattered over the vast Pacific Ocean are more than 20,000 islands, which are collectively known as Oceania. Some, such as New Guinea, are huge, but many are little more than specks in the ocean. Only a few thousand of the islands are inhabited.

This brightly-painted building is a Hindu temple in Nadi, Fiji.

Pacific peoples

The original inhabitants of the Pacific islands migrated from Southeast Asia about 7,000 years ago. They made long sea journeys and, over many generations, settled one group of islands after another. Later, in the 16th century, European explorers started to discover the Pacific islands. Colonists began to arrive, and by the 1800s many islands were under the control of other countries. Today, some Pacific islands are independent and others are still ruled by states such as the U.S.A., France and New Zealand.

Island groups

There are three main Pacific island groups: Melanesia, Polynesia and Micronesia. Polynesia means "many islands" and Micronesia means "small islands". Melanesia means "black islands"; it got its name because the people there tend to have darker skin than elsewhere in the Pacific.

These French Polynesian girls are wearing traditional flower garlands, known as leis.

Tourist paradise

Some of the Polynesian islands, such as Fiji, Tonga and Samoa, are among the most beautiful in the world. This, together with their tropical climate, makes them popular tourist destinations. Tourism brings money to the islands but too many tourists can also damage the environment.

ᜀᜁᜂᜃ Internet links ᜀᜁᜂᜃ

For links to the following websites, go to **www.usborne-quicklinks.com**

Website 1 Find out about the people of Fiji and other South Pacific islands with clickable maps and online activities.

Website 2 Feather money, masks and other items made by Pacific peoples.

Website 3 Explore Easter Island and see the unusual statues found there.

Island life

Some Pacific islanders live in towns, and work in large-scale industries such as fishing, mining or tourism. However, most have a traditional way of life in small villages, growing crops such as yams and sweet potatoes. Families keep pigs and chickens and, if they live near the coast, catch fish. People live in large, extended families, and community and religious life on the islands is important.

Testing weapons

Because of their remote locations, the Pacific islands have been used by the U.K., France and the U.S.A. for testing nuclear weapons. In 1946, an atom bomb was detonated on Bikini, one of the Marshall Islands in Micronesia, and many islanders had to leave their homes. Some underground tests continue today in French Polynesia, despite protests from conservation groups and local people worried about the environment.

This man is fishing by standing on a ledge jutting out just over the water and stabbing at fish with his spear.

Huts cluster along the beach on Mana Island, one of the many islands that make up Fiji.

USING INTERNET LINKS

Internet links

Throughout this book we have recommended websites where you can find out more about people around the world. To visit the sites, go to the **Usborne Quicklinks Website** where you will find links to all the sites.

1. Go to **www.usborne-quicklinks.com**
2. Type the keyword for this book: **peoples**
3. Type the page number of the link you want to visit.
4. Click on the links to go to the recommended sites.

Here are some of the things you can do on the websites recommended in this book:
• Explore a clickable map of the world and see famous sites, listen to local languages and send virtual postcards.
• Join an Arctic expedition and meet a team of huskies.
• Listen to songs of the Dogon people or learn Nigerian words by playing a matching game.
• Watch a "powhiri", a Maori welcome ceremony.
• Learn about religious festivals around the world then test your knowledge with online quizzes.

Site availability

The links in Usborne Quicklinks are regularly reviewed and updated, but occasionally you may get a message that a site is unavailable. This might be temporary, so try again later, or even the next day. Websites do occasionally close down and when this happens, we will replace them with new links in Usborne Quicklinks. Sometimes we add extra links too, if we think they are useful. So when you visit Usborne Quicklinks, the links may be slightly different from those described in your book.

COMPUTER NOT ESSENTIAL
If you don't have access to the Internet, don't worry. On its own, this book is a fascinating guide to peoples of the world.

Safety on the Internet

Ask your parent's or guardian's permission before you connect to the Internet and make sure you follow these simple rules:

• Never give out information about yourself, such as your real name, address, phone number or the name of your school.

• If a site asks you to log in or register by typing your name or email address, ask permission from an adult first.

What you need

To visit the websites you need a computer with an Internet connection and a web browser (the software that lets you look at information from the Internet). Some sites need extra programs (plug-ins) to play sound or show videos or animations.

If you go to a site and do not have the necessary plug-in, a message will come up on the screen. There is usually a link to click on to download the plug-in. For more information about plug-ins, go to Usborne Quicklinks and click on "Net Help".

Note for parents and guardians

The websites described in this book are regularly reviewed, but the content of a website may change at any time and Usborne Publishing is not responsible for the content on any website other than its own.

We recommend that children are supervised while on the Internet, that they do not use Internet chat rooms, and that you use Internet filtering software to block unsuitable material. Please ensure that your children read and follow the safety guidelines printed above. For more information, see the Net Help area on the Usborne Quicklinks Website.

INDEX

INDEX

ACKNOWLEDGEMENTS

Every effort has been made to trace the copyright holders of the material in this book. If any rights have been omitted, the publishers offer to rectify this in any subsequent edition, following notification. The publishers are grateful to the following organizations and individuals for their contributions and permission to reproduce material (t=top, m=middle, b=bottom, l=left, r=right):
Cover © Ric Ergenbright/CORBIS; **p1** © Kevin R. Morris/CORBIS; **p2** © Marc Garanger/CORBIS; **p4** (map) Oxford Cartographers; (globes) Laura Fearn; **p6** (tr) © Laura Dwight/CORBIS; (bl) © Rod Williams/Bruce Coleman; (br) Laura Fearn; **p7** (tl) © Frank Leather; Eye Ubiquitous/CORBIS; (br) © Studio Patellani/CORBIS; **p8** (tr) © Catherine Karnow/CORBIS; (b) © Pacific Stock/Bruce Coleman; (background) © Digital Vision; **p9** (tr) © Charles and Josette Lenars/CORBIS; (br) © Martin Dohrn/Bruce Coleman; **p10** © Phil Schermeister/CORBIS; **p12** (tr) Laura Fearn; (l) © Steve Kaufman/CORBIS; **p13** (t) Oxford Cartographers; (b) © Michael T. Sedam/CORBIS; **p14** (background) © Ron Watts/CORBIS; (tr) © Kevin Fleming/CORBIS; (bl) © Flip Schulke/CORBIS; **p15** (bl) © Douglas Peebles/CORBIS; (r) © Digital Vision; **p16** (main) © Marc Muench/CORBIS; (tr) © Gunter Marx/CORBIS; (br) © Lowell Georgia/CORBIS; **p17** (tr) © Michael Lewis/Bruce Coleman; (br) © Galen Rowell/CORBIS; **p18** (tr) © Gianni Dagli Orti/CORBIS; (b) Howard Allman; **p19** © Charles and Josette Lenars/CORBIS; **p20** (tr) © Bill Gentile/CORBIS; (bl) © Robert Francis/Hutchison; **p21** (t) Howard Allman; (br) © Danny Lehman/CORBIS; **p22** (tl+tr) Howard Allman; (b) © Bob Krist/CORBIS; **p23** (r) © Philip Gould/CORBIS; **p24** © Jeremy Horner/CORBIS; **p26** (tr) Laura Fearn; (br) Oxford Cartographers; (b) © Maurice Harvey/Hutchison; **p27** (r) © Alison Wright/CORBIS; **p28** (tr) © Jeremy Horner/CORBIS; (bl) © Pablo Corral V/CORBIS; (b) © Jeremy Horner/Hutchison; **p29** (br) © Sarah Errington/Hutchison; **p30** (tr) © Sesco Von Puttamer/Hutchison; (bl) © Wolfgang Kaehler/CORBIS; **p31** (tr) © Luiz Claudio Marigo/Bruce Coleman; (b) © The Purcell Team/CORBIS; **p32** (tr) © Jeremy Horner/Hutchison; (bl) © S. Molins/Hutchison; **p33** (tr) © Inge Yspeert/CORBIS; (b) © Edward Parker/Hutchison; **p34** (background) © Nicholas Devore/Bruce Coleman; (bl) © Will and Deni McIntyre/Tony Stone; **p35** (tr) © Edward Parker/Hutchison; (b) © Diego Lezama Orezzoli/CORBIS; **p36** © Fulvio Roiter/CORBIS; **p38** (tr) Laura Fearn; (bl) © Robbie Jack/CORBIS; **p39** Oxford Cartographers; **p40** (tl) Howard Allman; (main) © Bob Krist/CORBIS; **p41** (t) © Todd Gipstein/CORBIS; (br) © Elke Stolzenberg/CORBIS; **p42** (tr) © Greenpeace/Shirly; (bl) © Rethly Akos www.szoborpark.hu; **p43** (br) © Franz-Marc Frei/CORBIS; **p44** (main) © Jan Jordan; (tr) © Les Gibbon; Cordaiy Photo Library Ltd./CORBIS; (bl) © J. F. Causse/Tony Stone; **p45** (br) © Brian and Cherry Alexander; **p46** (tr) © European Parliament; (b) © Powerstock Zefa; **p47** (tl+tr) © European Communities; (br) © Peter Turnley/CORBIS; **p48** © Charles and Josette Lenars/CORBIS; **p50** (background) © Digital Vision; (tr) Laura Fearn; (b) © David Turnley/CORBIS; **p51** (t) Oxford Cartographers; **p52** (tr) © Margaret Courtney-Clarke/CORBIS; (b) © Adrian Arbib/CORBIS; **p53** (m) © Daniel Lainé/CORBIS; **p54** (background) © Christine Osborne/CORBIS; (tr) Ian Jackson; (bl) © J. Wright/Hutchison; **p55** (m) © Roger Wood/CORBIS; **p56** (main) © Sarah Errington/Hutchison; (l) © Mary Jellife/Hutchison; **p57** (tl) © Daniel Lainé/CORBIS; (tr) © Hutchison; **p58** (tr) © Digital Vision; (b) © Kevin Fleming/CORBIS; **p59** © Hutchison; **p60** (background) © Nevada Wier/CORBIS; (tr) Ian Jackson; (bl) © Peter Turnley/CORBIS; **p61** (tr) © Chris Hellier/CORBIS; (b) © Peter Johnson/CORBIS; **p62** (background) © Sarah Errington/Hutchison; (l) © Bruce Coleman Inc.; **p63** (tl) © Contemporary African Art Collection Limited/CORBIS; (bl) © Crispin Hughes/Hutchison; (r) © CORBIS; **p64** © Steve Raymer/CORBIS; **p66** (tr) Laura Fearn; (m) Oxford Cartographers; **p67** (background) © Dean Conger/CORBIS; (br) © Michael S. Yamashita/CORBIS; **p68** (background) © Alain Compost/Bruce Coleman; (bl) © Isabella Tree/Hutchison; **p69** (ml) © Kenneth Fischer/Bruce Coleman; (br) © Robin Constable/Hutchison; **p70** (background) © Digital Vision (tr) © Charles and Josette Lenars/CORBIS; (b) © Dave Saunders/Tony Stone; **p71** (tl) © Staffan Widstrand/Bruce Coleman; (br) © Christina Dodwell/Hutchison; **p72** (background) © B. Gerard/Hutchison; (tr) © Nik Wheeler/CORBIS; (bl) © Dave G. Houser/CORBIS; **p73** (bl) © Dean Conger/CORBIS; (r) Kevin Schafer/CORBIS; **p74** (tr) © Peter Turnley/CORBIS; (bl) Wally McNamee/CORBIS; **p75** (tl) © Christine Osborne/CORBIS; (r) Laura Fearn (b) © Kevin R. Morris/CORBIS; **p76** (background) © Wolfgang Kaehler/CORBIS; (tr) © David Clilverd/Hutchison; (bl) © Michael MacIntyre/Hutchison; **p77** (tr) © Catherine Karnow/CORBIS; (bl) © Jeremy Horner/Hutchison; **p78** (tr) © Paul Almasy/CORBIS; (bl) © Pacific Stock/Bruce Coleman; **p79** (main) © Gerald S. Cubitt/Bruce Coleman; (br) © Alain Compost/Bruce Coleman; **p80** © Earl and Nazima Kowall/CORBIS; **p82** (tl) Laura Fearn; (m) Oxford Cartographers; (b) © Paul Thompson; Eye Ubiquitous/CORBIS; **p83** (tl) © Bettmann/CORBIS; (tr) © Isabella Tree/Hutchison; **p84** (background) John Cancalosi/Bruce Coleman; (tr) © Patrick Ward/CORBIS; (bl) © Roger Ressmeyer/CORBIS; **p85** (tl) © Australian Picture Library/CORBIS; (br) © Charles and Josette Lenars/CORBIS; **p86** (background) © Gerald S. Cubitt/Bruce Coleman; (tr) © Robert Francis/Hutchison; **p87** (t) © Doug Armand/Tony Stone; (br) © Pacific Stock/Bruce Coleman; **p88** © Isabella Tree/Hutchison; **p89** (tl) © Chris Rainier/CORBIS; (br) © Fritz Prenzel/Bruce Coleman; **p90** (background) © Pacific Stock/Bruce Coleman; (tr) © Jan Butchofsky-Houser/CORBIS; (bl) © Pacific Stock/Bruce Coleman; **p91** (tr) © Jack Fields/CORBIS.